M000280682

Guide to
Cichlids

David E. Boruchowitz

This book is dedicated to my father, may he rest in peace.

Guide to Cichlids

Project Team
Editor: Brian Scott
Copy Editor: Phyllis DeGioia
Cover Design: Cándida Tómassini, Mary Ann Kahn
Design Team: Stephanie Krautheim, Patti Escabi

T.F.H. Publications
President/CEO: Glen S. Axelrod
Executive Vice President: Mark E. Johnson
Publisher: Christopher T. Reggio
Production Manager: Kathy Bontz

T.F.H. Publications, Inc.
One TFH Plaza
Third and Union Avenues
Neptune City, NJ 07753

Printed and bound in China,
05 06 07 08 09 1 3 5 7 9 8 6 4 2

Library of Congress Cataloging-in-Publication Data
Boruchowitz, David E.
Pocketprofessional guide to cichlids / David E. Boruchowitz. -- 1st ed.
p. cm.
Includes bibliographical references and index.
ISBN 0-7938-0584-8 (alk. paper)
1. Cichlids. I. Title. II. Title: Pocket professional guide to cichlids.
SF458.C5B68 2006
639.3'774--dc22
2006011269

This book has been published with the intent to provide accurate and authoritative information in regard to the subject matter within. While every precaution has been taken in preparation of this book, the author and publisher expressly disclaim responsibility for any errors, omissions, or adverse effects arising from the use or application of the information contained herein. The techniques and suggestions are used at the reader's discretion and are not to be considered a substitute for veterinary care. If you suspect a medical problem, consult your veterinarian.

The Leader In Responsible Animal Care For Over 50 Years!™
www.tfhpublications.com

Table of Contents

Introduction

It is one task to collect a mass of data like this book full of information about cichlids. It is quite another to organize the data in a meaningful way. That organization, however, is as important as the data, for without it, the data might as well not exist. Imagine the uselessness of a phone book in which the entries are arranged randomly.

Not all organizational schemes are of equal value in making the data accessible. Compare the relative usefulness of phone books whose entries are arranged by religious affiliation, alphabetically by street name, or by birthdates.

In the case of this book, a great deal of thought and planning has gone into the selection of an organizational paradigm. The driving image we kept in mind as we developed this book was of an aquarist standing in front of a dealer's tanks, paging through, trying to identify various fish and to decide which of them to purchase. A book that is a useful tool for that situation would serve equally well for a hobbyist looking for a new challenge to add to his or her fishroom, or for someone poring hungrily over an importer's list, or even just an aquarist wanting to learn more about the family Cichlidae as a whole.

PHYLOGENETIC ORGANIZATION

Without boring you with a list of all the rejected intermediate steps, it is worthwhile to mention the overall evolution of the final choice. The only acceptable scientific organization—alphabetically by genus—is sorely wanting if you're comparing a tank of *Amphilophus* with a tank of *Vieja*!

An alphabetic by species (rather than alphabetic by genus) listing is extremely useful as taxonomists ply their craft and genera come and go, but it creates an artificial chasm between *Apistogramma acrensis* and *A. urteagai*—even worse than the *Amphilophus/Vieja* gap, and it puts *Crenicichla wallacii* and *Gobiocichla wonderi* into artificial proximity.

A zoogeological organization is quite useful, since cichlids from the same area often resemble each other both in morphology and in husbandry requirements, though it still groups oscars and rams while it shoves apart North and South American cichlasomines. But this last scheme suggests a more useful one: phylogenetic organization. By organizing the cichlids of the world into evolutionary groups we can maximize the usefulness of this guide to aquarists wishing for whatever reason to research any particular species. In most cases this means in taxonomic terms grouping fish by tribe and alphabetically by genus within the tribe; any exceptions are noted in the text. Obviously, if we get bogged down in the minutiae of current taxonomic revision, our guide will quickly lose its usefulness. This is why we have chosen a compromise that entails following phylogeny—as manifested in taxonomy—as far as it is generally useful to the cichlid enthusiast, but then grouping fishes by criteria of importance to aquarists.

In addition, we hope that our readers will occasionally gain useful insight from the organization itself. In the same way that a ethnolinguist might glean helpful data by comparing a phone

Introduction

Herichthys carpintis **is one example of a species that has changed genera several times and therefore is not easily located in older texts.**

directory's listings for "Cohen," "Kahn," and "Katz," an aquarist might learn something about cichlids by our grouping of Indian and Malagasy species or by the inclusion of species from two continents in our treatment of cichlasomine cichlids.

We admit up front that our scheme has holes. Even the tightest taxonomies leak, and any treatment of the cichlids is going to be like a hastily packed suitcase with a tie hanging out of one end and a shirt cuff out of the other. We know that we have some polyphyletic groups, that some of our groupings may contain animals related by convergence—or even coincidence— rather than phylogeny. But this is where the compromise comes in; we have two goals: scientific accuracy and hobbyist utility. When the first no longer serves the second, it must yield.

Using This Guide

Obviously, if you know a cichlid's name, it is very easy to find it in this book—look it up in the alphabetic index. If however, you know only that the fish in question looks like an *Oreochromis*, or has the general appearance of a lamprologine, or appears suspiciously like a West African riverine species with which you are familiar already, you can use the table of contents or even just skim through the book to the general area, then scan for your target. This is the utility that we have strived to incorporate. The information in this section will help you get maximum use from the book. Now, let's take a look at each of the components of our species entries to see how you can use it most efficiently

SCIENTIFIC NAMES

The first entry for each species is the scientific name. We have strived to give the most accurate, up-to-date name for each fish. But it's important to understand that even if all known species were described already, there would still be enormous revision underway, and if no more cichlids were ever discovered, their taxonomy would still need major revision. This is so because of the misunderstandings that researchers have had for years, which are just now beginning to be fixed properly. This is mostly due to the use of DNA sequencing and identifying species based on the results of comparing the DNA fingerprint to other known species. As it turns out, we do have DNA data available at our disposal, many fish in the trade have yet to be described, and new cichlids are still being discovered.

Essentially, this means that any book will be out of date before the ink on its pages has dried. Rather than take a defeatist attitude, however, we have tried to provide the most up-to-date and accurate information, without getting sidetracked by unresolved details. Recent developments and interesting problems are duly noted. Because of our unique organization, however, the usefulness of this book will remain high even when some names get changed—a real advantage over a simple alphabetical listing. If a cichlid's name changes, even from A to Z, in this book it will only move up or down within its group, not from one end of the book to the other.

AUTHOR & DATE

Second in each listing is the author and date for the species. Keep in mind that this is the *original* description. It is important to note whether or not the information is in parentheses; if it is, the name listed is not the original. Why does this matter? First, it will assist you if you wish to research anything about the fish's taxonomy; if the name is in parentheses, you know you're looking for a different name in the original description. But it also helps you to gain an integral understanding of the taxonomy of your favorite fishes.

For example, you might know that there has been some uncertainty about the genera *Lamprologus* and *Neolamprologus*, and that several species were transferred from the first to the second genus. Then you see then entry: *Neolamprologus cylindricus* STAECK & SEEGERS 1986 without parentheses. This tells you that this species was originally described *after* the split of *Neolamprologus* from *Lamprologus*.

Similarly, when you see *Paretroplus nourissati* (ALLGAYER 1998) with parentheses, you note that despite its recent original description—1998—this species has already been reassigned. (See the entry to find out what happened.)

TRADE NAMES

What about common names? There is a very prevalent belief that there is a one-to-one relationship between scientific names and common names, but this is completely wrong. People say things like, "what is the common name for *Archocentrus myrnae*?", but the only valid question is, "what is **a** common name for *Archocentrus myrnae*?" You will hear statements like "a firemouth cichlid is a *Thorichthys meeki*," but this is not a true statement. Why? Because there are no standards for, or regulation of common names, and no way of validly assigning common names to particular species.

Since there is no standard for common names, and since they are sometimes used idiosyncratically by distributors and retailers, it is impossible to say that any common name is right or wrong for any species; all one can do is note the relative frequency of one name over another in common usage.

A second problem is that different breeders may produce under the same common name varieties which are of very different genetic backgrounds. This underscores the fact that the reality of the hobby and of the trade is that any cichlid labeled by just a common name is at least of suspect heredity and quite likely a hybrid. While it is generally true that a cichlid labeled "Malawi peacock" is descended from species in the genus *Aulonocara*, even this genus-level naming is not universally correct—the very popular "OB peacock," for example, has other generic ancestry as well.

So, to maintain accuracy, we are not assigning common names to the fishes in this book, but, to maintain hobbyist utility, we do list trade names for those species which are frequently labeled with such names as long as there is some uniformity to the application of those names.

Please keep in mind that even if only one trade name is given for a particular species, we are absolutely *not* saying that there is a one-to-one correspondence between that name and the scientific name with which it is found! All we are indicating is that people tend to use that common name for that species. It also could be used for another species, and this same species could also be known by any number of other common names.

One final complication: The use of scientific binomials as common names is prevalent in the trade. Huh? Well, it's a case of a little knowledge being dangerous. A fish labeled "*Pseudotropheus zebra*" could be any of dozens of actual species, or, regrettably, a hybrid of several. Labels can be applied anywhere in the chain from breeder or importer to retailer, and it would be rare indeed if a label were applied by a trained taxonomist! So, keep in mind that the correct identification of a particular fish is never guaranteed.

This is why we've worked so hard for accuracy in this book, and why we give little significance to common names. If you are mistakenly sold a fish under the wrong scientific name, you can certainly use this book to help you find the right Latin name by comparing photos and descriptions. But if you buy a certain fish whose label matches a trade name in this book, there is absolutely no guarantee that you have purchased the species with which we list that trade name. In short, we cannot control, know, or foresee how common names will be applied.

SIZE

The size listed is understood as the maximum for the species. It is not, however, an absolute, for a variety of reasons. Not all

The marbled convict (*Cryptoheros nigrofasciatum*) is a captive-produced OB color morph of the zebra convict cichlid (*C. nigrofasciatum*).

members of a species grow to the same size—just look at people. In some cases, captive care may contribute to growth that is less or more than typical in the wild. And sometimes our knowledge is incomplete, and the maximum size we have listed for a species is based on too small a sample to encompass the whole population. Also, like most cold-blooded animals, fish can continue to grow—albeit very slowly—throughout their lives, so very old fish can be very big for their species. Use the size we list as a guideline, not an absolute. Also keep in mind that in many cichlid species males get considerably larger than females. In addition, almost all species of cichlid mature sexually long before they reach maximum size, so it is possible to breed the largest species at much more manageable sizes by using young stock.

Altolamprologus compressiceps **is a perfect example of a cichlid species where the males grow larger, to 6 inches (15 cm), than the females, to 3 inches (7.5 cm).**

DIETARY NOTES

In the husbandry sections of each chapter we discuss diet and requirements for the group. Thus, under each individual entry we only note any information you need to apply the advice given for captive husbandry. Check the general section for details.

REMARKS

A brief review of pertinent information about the species appears in this section. This may cover natural range if specific or otherwise noteworthy, history in the hobby, special requirements, or breeding information. The first listing in a genus often contains general information for that genus, so always check the first species.

Using This Guide

PHOTOS

Photos are as important, or in some cases more important than text. They can often give you instant identification, but occasionally they do the opposite, which is also very useful. There are species that are extremely difficult to tell apart in photos. When you see several pages of fish that look the same, you realize that even the experts can have a tough time, and, you understand that just because a fish is labeled doesn't mean the label is correct.

WHAT ISN'T INCLUDED IN INDIVIDUAL ENTRIES

Many other references contain entries we omit for each species. General information about natural range, husbandry, breeding, and diet would be redundant in this book, since this information is given for each group before the species are listed. Remember, to get maximum value from this book, don't just read a species entry, read the introductory material and the entry for the first species in the genus. Because of the way we've arranged the content, it is also very useful to read several entries before and after the one which you're investigating—something that wouldn't be too helpful in a listing where *Altolamprologus* is next to *Amphilophus*!

Symbol Legend

| 7.8 | 8.0 | + | **pH strip** = Indicates the best pH range for the species. |

Full Sun = Indicates the species prefers brightly illuminated aquariums.

Half Sun = Indicates the species prefers dimly illuminated aquariums.

Thermometer = Indicates the optimal temperature range for each species.

21.1   26.6   32.2   37.7 °C
70   80   90   100 °F

Chapter I

Why Cichlids?

Since you're reading this book, chances are you have already been bitten by the cichlidophile bug, and your answer to the question "Why cichlids?" is a vociferous, "Why not!" The sense of this question that we are addressing here, however, is the biological one: how do we account for the family Cichlidae, its provenance, diversity, and complexity?

GENERAL BIOLOGY

Cichlids specialize in generalization. A measure of their success is seen in that cichlid species are found in tropical and subtropical areas, exist in fresh, brackish, and marine habitats, can be herbivorous, omnivorous, or carnivorous, reproduce as substrate spawners or mouthbrooders, and range in size from tiny shelldwellers to 3-foot (100-cm) giants. The radiation of cichlid species—in some cases in extremely short periods of time—is one of the most fascinating aspects of the family.

Much of their success is due to the preadaptations ancestral cichlids brought with them into new environments. For example, the pharyngeal jaws of cichlids are an adaptation permitting the oral jaws to be used only for food procurement and not food processing. This has enabled cichlids to develop extremely diverse mouth types. In fact, plasticity in exploiting food sources may be the single most important key to cichlids' success.

The jaguar guapote *(Parachromis managuensis)* is an accomplished piscivorous cichlid that uses its protrusable jaws to the maximum advantage.

In Lake Malawi we find a remarkable niche exploitation by cichlids which enables sympatric species to utilize completely different foods. Some comb algae strands, scraping *aufwuchs* but leaving the algae, which other species scrape off the rocks. Yet others remove algal growth from plant leaves. There are cichlids that grab lake flies from just above the surface of the water and cichlids that snatch plankton out of the water column. There are even species that mimic their prey, joining their schools to have a ready supply of tasty scales, and there are those that feign death, waiting on their sides on the substrate until curious scavengers venture near enough for them to be grabbed.

Cichlid parental behavior is also complex and varied, and it covers a broad spectrum: monogamy, polygamy, and polygyny (including harems and lekking), using substrate brooding, delayed mouthbrooding, and immediate mouthbrooding. We also find sibling brood care, colony breeding, and even mouthbrooding species that spawn in the water column with no substrate for egg deposition.

Another cichlid preadaptation that certainly gave them a distinct advantage in many environments with high predation pressure is the fact that their swimbladders are filled with gas produced by a specialized gland. This means that cichlid fry do not have to surface to fill their bladders, making it much easier for their parents to keep them safe.

BIOGEOGRAPHY

Cichlids are native to North America, South America, Africa, and Asia, with the latter having a mere three species restricted to India and Sri Lanka. On the other three continents, this family is widespread and diverse, with 1500 to 2000 species in total.

The common firemouth *(Thorichthys meeki)* is classified as a monogamous bi-parental substratum spawning cichlid.

Central to a discussion of the biogeography of Cichlidae is the separation of Madagascar from Africa. Timelines based on fossils seem to place the evolution of the first cichlids after Madagascar broke off from Africa, though there is certainly no wealth of proto-cichlid and early cichlid fossils. Thus, the fossil record does not yield definitive answers about the origin of the family, and ongoing DNA analysis cannot yet give us the big picture.

Continental drift itself can be used to frame a timeline of cichlid evolution. Critics of this approach argue that the recent marine origin of these fish has left many of them with considerable tolerance for salinity; thus, as the continents began to drift apart, cichlids could have crossed the widening seas, maintaining genetic contact longer than originally thought.

A problem with this line of reasoning is that no cichlid has ever been found in the predator-rich open ocean (though many are found near shore, on reefs), and there is good reason to

Malagasy cichlids, like this *Paratilapia* species, are generally considered basal (most primitive) cichlids.

believe that, lacking a pelagic, planktonic larval stage, cichlids could maintain any sort of genetic ties across seas.

So, the problem for any cichlid discussion is that if the earliest cichlids appeared *after* Madagascar-India broke off from Africa—or even after Africa and South America split—then how did cichlids get into all three? Of all the data, the morphological and DNA analyses provide strong evidence that Malagasy cichlids are basal (most primitive), that their relationship with Indian species is consistent with the Madagascar-India split as we understand it now, and that the differentiation of American cichlids from African species occurred after these two continents separated.

An intriguing idea recently proposed is that Cichlidae may not be monophyletic, and this obviously could solve the continental drift problem. If, for example, Malagasy and Indian cichlids form one clade and African and American cichlids another, the appearance of the latter after Madagascar-India split from Africa is no longer a concern.

For our purposes here, we recognize that either way, Malagasy cichlids are living fossils, with their progenitors either ancestral to (Figure 1) or polyphyletic with (Figure 2) African and American species.

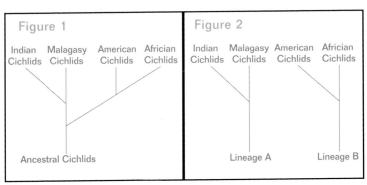

Figure 1

Indian Cichlids   Malagasy Cichlids   American Cichlids   Africian Cichlids

Ancestral Cichlids

Figure 2

Indian Cichlids   Malagasy Cichlids   American Cichlids   Africian Cichlids

Lineage A   Lineage B

Chapter 2

Taxonomy

Not only are cichlid species numerous (currently thought to be somewhere between 1500 and 3500), a vast number of them are new to science in the last half century alone. It is not surprising, therefore, that their taxonomy is in a perpetual state of flux. It is important for serious aquarists to understand some aspects of taxonomy without worrying about all of the intricacies.

Most cichlid hobbyists are familiar, even conversant, with scientific names. Aquarists use specific names even more readily than generic names, because much of the taxonomic revision that goes on involves genera, and species names change less frequently. The "common" name for many cichlids is simply the species name assimilated into everyday speech, e.g., "nics," "umbies," "brichardi," etc.

A Slippery Definition

Attempts at defining a species are fueled by the obvious—everyone "knows" what a species is. It is typical for a language to have specific names, that is, words to refer to various local species. Young children usually have no difficulty telling various species apart, even when the amount of polymorphism within a species is great (e.g., domestic dogs).

The problem arises when we try for a rigid scientific definition. The ongoing scientific debate is of limited concern to us as hobbyists. Species are an observable fact of biological reality; organisms exist as individual members of a population which protects its gene pool from excessive variation by limiting reproduction. The same dynamic which makes sexual reproduction so successful can also reduce the viability of the next generation.

LIMITING VARIABILITY

Acquired characteristics are what fit a species into its niche. Typically, long evolutionary paths are involved in the acquisition of certain traits. A species obviously benefits if its members do not interbreed with organisms that lack these traits. In fact, in an ideal world, in which every genetic trait always had positive survival value, the best situation would be one of zero variability.

Of course, this world is anything but ideal, and every species, every organism, has an accumulation of genetic material that is of negative survival value. In addition, the stresses and the opportunities which living things face, change over space and time, meaning that traits which were once useful can become liabilities, and vice versa.

Meiotic sexual reproduction is a biological answer to the world's non-ideal state. With a doubled genetic inventory, each individual receives half its genetic material from each parent. For any given trait, these two halves can be the same or different. For many physical traits in a given species, all individuals of that species have at least one gene that is the same—the normal or wild-type gene. They can also carry latent genes mutations in half of the genetic material which are not expressed in the presence of the wild-type other half.

Thus, a negative trait inherited from one parent can be masked or offset by the normal gene of the other parent. On the other hand, such latent traits can prove beneficial when conditions change, so the fact that they occasionally combine—when provided by each parent—allows maximum use of genetic variability in the population.

Thus, maximum viability is obtained when a species preserves its hard-won adaptations by preventing genetic influx from too-dissimilar organisms, preserving just enough variation in its biotype to maintain genetic health.

AN IMPORTANT DISTINCTION

This concept of species is different from the taxon called "species," and although the two are related, the former is a biological reality while the latter is a human construct—a systematic reality. The

Symphysodon aequifasciata, wild "blue" discus, a textbook example of genetic variability, with differently colored populations being all the same species.

biological species is always changing, evolving. It can have ill-defined boundaries, with a certain frequency of natural hybridization occurring at the limits of its range. Our observations of natural species are necessarily like flash snapshots of an evolutionary dynamic, and we may come upon a well-established biology, or upon one in a state of flux (e.g., Lake Victorian cichlids).

LAKE VICTORIA

Although the claim that the hundreds of endemic cichlid species in Lake Victoria evolved in a mere 12,000 years has recently come under dispute, it is clear that cichlid speciation in this lake was nevertheless rapid and rampant by normal evolutionary standards.

One of the mechanisms of this speciation was mate selection. The females of a great many polygamous maternal mouthbrooding species are drably similar, while the raucously colored males represent an enormous variety of patterns.

Removed from the lake, where many geological and biological constraints assist ethological limits on hybridization,

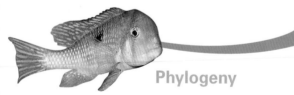

Phylogeny

Cichlidae is placed under the suborder Labroidei, which includes the surf perches (Embiotocidae), the damselfishes (Pomacentridae), the wrasses (Labridae), the parrotfishes (Scaridae), and others. Many of the fascinating relationships among the various cichlid subgroups will be discussed in the following chapters.

Cichlid speciation in Lake Victoria is very rapid and clearly rampant by "normal" evolutionary standards.

these cichlids are frustratingly interfertile—such that many aquarium strains are hopelessly hybridized, even between genera. Their recent speciation has not provided enough time for rigid barriers to hybridization to evolve; the behavioral and ecological barriers suffice in the lake, but not in aquaria.

This has had an unusual consequence in terms of current conditions in Lake Victoria. Predation by the introduced *Lates nilotica* is certainly responsible for the extinction of dozens of species of cichlids, but agricultural and urban runoff and the subsequent eutrophication and silting of the lake place yet more stress on the beleaguered ecosystem. The now-turbid water presents a definite obstacle to mate recognition among surviving cichlids.

We are probably seeing speciation as new breeding populations form. Since some colors and patterns are more visible than others under the murky conditions, females have fewer and different choices to make, based on only the most salient features of the males' coloration.

Chapter 3

Region 1
Madagascar
& India

We begin our phylogenetic survey of the cichlids of the world on the biologically unique island-continent of Madagascar, once part of the southern supercontinent of Gondwana, which began to break up about 165 million years ago (mya). At that time Madagascar was located between current-day Kenya and India. About 120 mya Madagascar reached its current position off the east coast of Africa, while India broke off from Madagascar and began its trek toward Asia about 90 mya. South America and Africa, however, remained joined until sometime around 50 mya.

Current understanding based on DNA analysis shows the relationship among cichlids in this area as in Figure 3.

Malagasy Cichlids

Living fossils, having survived for millions of years unaffected by changes in fish populations on the mainland, Malagasy cichlids are disappearing from our planet even as we watch. Heavy fishing pressure, loss of habitat, and the introduction of alien species conspire to eliminate these species, and some—perhaps many—have already been lost forever.

The taxonomy of this group is as uncertain as their fate. While assignment to genus is fairly straightforward for most of

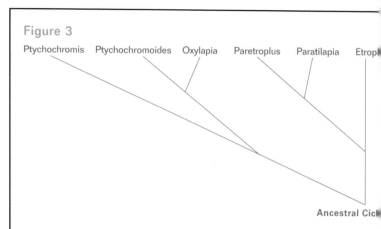

Figure 3

Ptychochromis Ptychochromoides Oxylapia Paretroplus Paratilapia Etrop▮

Ancestral Cic▮

them, deciding species status for their highly variable populations is another matter. Since conservation should be foremost on the mind of any aquarist keeping these animals, it behooves us to keep different types in separate breeding programs. Whether we are preserving local races or different species, such caution will permit future generations to be able to enjoy the fullness of Malagasy cichlid variability—at least in captivity.

Natural History & Captive Husbandry

Many Malagasy habitats are quite variable, becoming more saline during droughts, and changing with seasonal rains and floods. Cichlids from these habitats tend to do very well in water that is not too extreme in pH or hardness, though water that is near neutral pH with moderate hardness is the natural environment for most of them. Although there are some reports of certain species surviving cold water in Madagascar's mountains, the names used in these accounts are suspect given current taxonomy, so it is best to consider all of these cichlids truly tropical, with temperatures around 80°F (27.5°C) ideal. Better safe than sorry.

Being primitive in form, these are omnivorous and opportunistic feeders, and they can thrive on a well-balanced diet of commercially available foods which includes plenty of vegetable matter. They are large and heavy feeders, yet they require excellent water conditions, so heavy-duty filtration and frequent, large water changes are in order.

Managing aggression is extremely important. The liberal use of hiding places and visual barriers is mandatory. The use of incomplete barriers for breeding pairs is very often indicated, as males are typically much larger than the females.

Captive breeding is of utmost importance with all of these fishes. It is realistic rather than pessimistic to understand that there is little hope for Madagascar's indigenous flora and fauna. Conservation efforts are vital, but we cannot rely on them to save the cichlids. If we do not establish viable and self-sustaining captive populations of these fish, there is little chance of them being around for long.

A plaguing requirement for many of these species, which may or may not diminish as captive strains are produced, is the need for enormous amounts of space to even initiate spawning. Often, even when a pair spawns in an aquarium, they eat the spawn immediately.

Etroplinae

The cichlids in the subfamily Etroplinae comprise five genera on Madagascar and one in Asia. Like almost all endemic lifeforms of Madagascar, the cichlids there are on the brink of extinction. In fact, a couple of species are considered extinct, and it is quite possible that others have gone extinct before becoming known to science. They are all biparental substrate spawners.

Oxylapia polli
KIENER & MAUGÉ 1966

Size: 5 inches (13 cm) TL.

Dietary Notes: Omnivorous.

Remarks: Known locally as *songatana*, this is a much sought after reophilic species in a monotypic genus. It is extremely aggressive and requires a very large tank with rock or wood hiding places. We are aware of no successful captive spawnings of this cichlid, one which frustrated even the master Jean-Claude Nourissat with his outdoor pools. Wild pairs defend 6-foot-plus diameter territories, so most aquaria are obviously too small even for one pair.

Paratilapia bleekeri
SAUVAGE 1891

| 7.2 | 7.4 | 7.6 |

Size: 12 inches (30 cm) TL.
Dietary Notes: Omnivorous.
Remarks: This genus went from a catchall for many African species to monotypic, and now it contains a couple species, with several variable populations under study, so there may be additional species added. There is great confusion in the hobby as to whether the large- and small-spotted cichlids are one or two species. This is the traditional designation for the large-spotted fish. Heavily over-fished and facing invading tilapia and bass in the wild, these fish, known as *marakely* or *fony*, are firmly established in the hobby and bred commercially. These two popular spotted cichlids are considered by many to be "Malagasy oscars" in their behavior and appeal. They are much less aggressive than most of their compatriots.

Paratilapia polleni
BLEEKER 1868

| 7.2 | 7.4 | 7.6 |

Size: 11 inches (28 cm) TL.

Dietary Notes: Omnivorous.

Remarks: This is the small-spotted fish, known locally as *fiamanga*. Whether *P. bleekeri* is a variant of *P. polleni* or a congener, the two fish are very similar and quite variable geographically, and there are several *Paratilapia* populations in Madagascar that may be assigned to these species, or to new ones. All variants should be kept in separate breeding programs. They may breed when they measure as little as 2 inches (5 cm), and their eggs do not adhere to the substrate, but clump in the nest.

Paratilapia sp. "Fianarantsoa"
UNDESCRIBED TO DATE

Trade Name: Green Face *Paratilapia*

Size: 12 inches (30 cm) TL.

Dietary Notes: Omnivorous.

Remarks: This interesting *Paratilapia* species remains undescribed. Growing slightly larger than its conspecifics, they are only suitable for large aquariums. Females of *P.* sp. "Fianarantsoa" tend to be more elongated compared to females of both *P.* sp "small spot" and *P.* sp. "large spot." There is undoubtedly much work that needs to be completed on *Paratilapia* as a whole, and on many levels before we can have a better understanding of the actual differences between the species. Their care in aquariums should be modeled after other cichlids of the group and quite a lot of vegetable material should be included in their diet.

Paretroplus dambabe
SPARKS 2002

Size: 6 inches (15 cm) TL.
Dietary Notes: Omnivorous.
Remarks: A beautiful and almost-extinct Malagasy cichlid. Dedicated aquarists should establish breeding programs for this and other species.

Paretroplus damii
BLEEKER 1868

Size: 8 inches (20 cm) TL.

Dietary Notes: Omnivorous.

Remarks: The *damba* is native to the northwestern region of Madagascar. Adults have a yellow bank on their backs that turns reddish during spawning. The eggs are usually deposited on a vertical surface, and this species has been bred in captivity. They do well in aquariums that contain other large, peaceful fishes, but during spawning, males may become intolerant of each other. Large adults are best kept in very large aquariums with excellent water quality.

Paretroplus kieneri
Arnoult 1960

Size: 5 inches (13 cm) TL.

Dietary Notes: Omnivorous.

Remarks: The *kotsovato* is calico in color and distinctive in appearance. These fish are quite attractive as juveniles, but the color fades somewhat in the adult. They are bred fairly regularly in aquaria, and they are the smallest in the genus, which makes them ideal for an aquarist not ready for the challenge of some of the more difficult species.

Paretroplus maculatus
KIENER & MAUGÉ 1966

Size: 8 inches (20 cm) TL.

Dietary Notes: Omnivorous, needs about equal amounts of plant and animal matter.

Remarks: Known locally as *damba taché* (Malagasy-French for "spotted damba"), *P. maculatus* is critically endangered. It is also extremely rare in the hobby, and hobbyists who have extra tank space are encouraged to keep these beautiful fish while they still have the chance. This is an extremely showy fish and a 200- or 300-gallon (756 – 1134 l) aquarium with a half dozen specimens makes a spectacular display.

Paretroplus maromandia
SPARKS & REINTHAL, 1999

Size: 10 inches (25 cm) TL.

Dietary Notes: Omnivorous.

Remarks: This new species is very rare in the hobby, but its bright red scales on the bellies between the dark bars are sure to capture many aquarists' attention. Hopefully, captive breeding projects will increase its availability to hobbyists and public collections alike.

Paretroplus menarambo
ALLGAYER 1996

Size: 10 inches (25 cm) TL.

Dietary Notes: Omnivorous.

Remarks: The *damba menarambo* (red tail) is extremely endangered, but it is being bred by aquarists in the United States and is becoming more common in the hobby at least. Occasionally a male will spawn with two females on one rock. This is a beautiful fish, and keeping an aquarium bustling with these brutes will be a rewarding experience.

41

Paretroplus nourissati
(ALLGAYER 1998)

| 7.2 | 7.4 | 7.6 |

Size: 6 inches (15 cm) TL.

Dietary Notes: Omnivorous.

Remarks: This is the almost-mythical "lamena," originally described as *Lamena nourissati*. The local name *lamena* means "red one," and this reophilic cichlid is extremely colorful, especially when in breeding dress, with the males bright red-orange and the females yellow. Spawnings have been reported, but they are still not common. The fish that became known as *Lamena* sp. "blue lips," has been described as *P. tsimoly* (q.v.).

Paretroplus petiti
PELLEGRIN 1929

| 7.2 | 7.4 | 7.6 |

Size: 10 inches (25 cm) TL.

Dietary Notes: Omnivorous.

Remarks: The *kotso* is a beautiful fish, though it is quite drab until it reaches about 6 inches, when it develops the red patterns on the sides. This fish is being bred in captivity, so hopefully the supply will increase.

43

Paretroplus polyactis
BLEEKER 1878

Size: 12 inches (30 cm) TL.

Dietary Notes: Omnivorous.

Remarks: The local name *masovoatoaka* refers to the red eyes of someone drunk on rum. Probably because this species often enters brackish water, it is nowhere near as threatened as other Malagasy cichlids. The largest in its genus, it is not well known in the hobby.

Ptychochromis oligacanthus
(BLEEKER 1868)

Size: 10 inches (25 cm) TL.

Dietary Notes: Omnivorous.

Remarks: Is there one species or are there more? Two other species, *P. grandidieri* SAUVAGE 1882 and *P. inornatus* SPARKS 2002, have been described, though the first is now considered a synonym of *P. oligacanthus*. There are several phenotypes over a large area that may or may not be assigned to new species. Even on the island of Nosy Be, where the local *tsipoy* has been considered *Ptychochromis nossibeensis*, there is a distinct phenotype in each of the nine crater lakes, all of which may be separate species. Various native names apply to fishes considered by some to be *P. oligacanthus*—*tsipoy*, *juba*, *saroy*, *saro*, etc. There is a yellow form, which has been bred in captivity, and a blue form with red fins, as well as other colorations.

Ptychochromoides katria
RHEINTHAL & STIASSNY 1997

| 7.2 | 7.4 | 7.6 |

Size: 6 inches (15 cm) TL.
Dietary Notes: Omnivorous.
Remarks: Although threatened, this fish, known as *katria*, is holding its own against tilapia in the Nosivolo River. It is less aggressive than most Malagasy cichlids, smaller than most others, and has been bred repeatedly—which hopefully should soon make it well established in the hobby.

Asian Cichlids

These living fossils have preserved many traits of the earliest cichlids, including a predilection for brackish conditions. The one genus confined to India and Sri Lanka is *Etroplus*, with three species in it; these primitive cichlids are not common in the hobby, though *E. maculatus* has held marginal popularity for many decades. Its preference for brackish water, especially for breeding, has probably kept it from the mainstream. However, there currently seems to be a surge of interest in this genus.

Natural History & Captive Husbandry

These fishes are fairly peaceful cichlids, especially when compared to their cousins in Madagascar. They are, of course, territorial when spawning, but otherwise they are suitable tankmates for most robust fishes. They are not able to stand up to pugnacious cichlids.

The first species, *E. canarensis*, was virtually unknown in the hobby until a few years ago, when the first imports were made. So far, this fish has not been reported from brackish waters, but its two congeners have a preference for brackish conditions, especially for spawning. You should maintain them in a specific gravity between 1.005 and 1.010. Use a marine salt mix, not plain sodium chloride.

Etroplus maculatus is one of the most popular Asian cichlids.

Etroplus canarensis
DAY 1877

| 7.2 | 7.4 | 7.6 |

Size: 4.5 inches (11 cm) TL
Dietary Notes: Omnivorous.
Remarks: While the other two species are found widely in India and Sri Lanka, this fish is restricted to southern Karnataka in India. This rare-in-the-hobby cichlid is now being imported from suppliers in India. Breeding success has been sporadic, but hopefully soon it will be more generally available. While its two congeners are regularly found in brackish waters such as estuaries and lagoons—where they breed—this species is apparently restricted to freshwater habitats.

Etroplus maculatus
(BLOCH 1795)

| 7.2 | 7.4 | 7.6 |

21.1   26.6   32.2   37.7 °C
70   80   90   100 °F

Trade Names: Orange chromide, red chromide, yellow chromide.

Size: 3 inches (8 cm) TL.

Dietary Notes: Omnivorous.

Remarks: In nature, this cichlid inhabits small streams and lagoons, where it feeds on fish fry, insects, and other small organisms. They occasionally move into estuaries where they are subjected to tidal influences and brackish water. These fish do well in aquariums with other peaceful cichlids and fishes large enough to fend for themselves. Aquarium strains have been developed that lack the black spotting and intensify the red coloration and are sold as "red chromides." There appears to be an unusual symbiosis between this fish and its much-larger congener *E. suratensis*. Juvenile *maculatus* act as cleaners for their larger cousins, but in turn, schools of *maculatus* raid the nests of *suratensis* and feast on the eggs and fry.

49

Etroplus suratensis
(BLOCH 1790)

Trade Name: Green chromide.

Size: 18 inches (45 cm) TL.

Dietary Notes: Strongly herbivorous; make sure to include green foods.

Remarks: The green chromide has been observed breeding in both fresh and brackish water conditions. They are found in large rivers, reservoirs, lagoons, and estuaries. In captivity, they need large aquariums with peaceful but large tankmates. They fare best when kept in schools of six or more. Many hobbyists keep large scats or monos with them as dither fishes. The cleaning behavior by *E. maculatus*—once the hosts are too large to eat—may explain the close sympatry of these two species.

Subfamilies

Now that we have completed our overview of the small, basal subfamily Etroplinae, and before we head back to Africa, let's take a look at all the subfamilies in Cichlidae. The vast bulk of this book will deal with two subfamilies, Pseudocrenilabrinae in Africa and Cichlinae in the New World. Neither of them is basal, however, for their parts of the world.

In that invertebrate evolution, extant forms which are considered basal, represent vestiges—leftover hangers—on who maintained ancestral features while all around them sibling groups radiated in various directions. In Africa, this position is held by the subfamily Heterochromidinae, and in South America by the subfamily Retroculinae. Both are typically extremely small in number of species.

Heterochromis multidens belongs to the subfamily Heterochromidinae.

Heterochromidinae

This family comprises a single species. Although some DNA studies place this cichlid in a Neotropical clade, Farias, Orti, and Meyer found conclusively that it was the base of the African cichlid radiation.

Heterochromis multidens
(PELLEGRIN 1900)

Size: 12 inches (30 cm) TL.

Dietary Notes: Probably omnivorous.

Remarks: Widespread in the Congo Basin, this large, rather drab cichlid is not at all common in the hobby. It should be kept and probably breeds like a substratum spawning tilapia.

Retroculinae

This subfamily, and its single tribe Retroculini, contains three species in one genus. They occur in the Amazon Basin and are found in rapids. They show a definite affinity to the geophagines, especially in the blue spangling on the bodies.

In aquariums, they can be very aggressive towards each other. Additionally, they may prove difficult to feed. Offer small live foods at first, then switch them over to a prepared diet.

Retroculus lapidifer
(Castelnau 1855)
Size: 8 inches (20 cm) TL.

Retroculus lapidifer
(Castelnau 1855)
Size: 8 inches (20 cm) TL.

Retroculus xinguensis
Gosse 1971
Size: 6 inches (15 cm) TL.

Retroculus xinguensis
Gosse 1971
Size: 6 inches (15 cm) TL.

Chapter 4

Region 2
Lake Malawi

About 500 endemic species of cichlids fill the niches of Lake Malawi, more than in any other lake in the world. Their taxonomy is fogged by two major problems: the persistent volume of newly discovered species and the extreme difficulty in deciding species status for many populations. The situation is even more complicated for hobbyists, since these fish will breed indiscriminately in captivity, meaning that in most cases only populations for which original collection data is available and which are assuredly unhybridized can be considered natural varieties.

All endemic Malawi cichlids are considered to be descended from a single ancestral haplochromine species (thus all Malawi species are in the tribe Haplochromini), and their adaptive radiation is one of the marvels of nature. All are maternal mouthbrooders.

THE MBUNA

Perhaps best known among Malawi cichlids are the *mbuna*. The native name, meaning "rockfish," is used for a dozen genera of small rock-dwelling cichlids that frenziedly defend territories among the rocks, feeding mostly on algae. Some people divide off "peacocks" of the genus *Aulonocara*, from other open-water cichlids, often called *utaka*, though that term strictly applies only to planktonivorous cichlids of the genus *Copadichromis*. In common usage, *mbuna* now often refers to the smaller, more specialized cichlids found in rocky and sandy zones, as opposed to the larger, more primitive, haplochromis-like, open-water species.

Rock-dwelling cichlids are noted for their frequent polymorphism, with BB (blue barred) males most common. O or OB (orange, orange blotch) forms are usually female. In some, the male is unbarred blue, while the female is white, and just about any permutation in this system is found in at least one population. While admittedly grounds for much ethological and evolutionary discussion, this situation is also greatly appreciated by aquarists, who delight in the variation shown in a given species of cichlid. Although "*mbuna*" has no taxonomic validity, we follow common hobbyist use here as a catchall category for smaller cichlids associated with rocky zones in the lake.

Natural History & Husbandry

All Malawi cichlids need similar water conditions, namely tropical, moderately hard, and basic. Most are quite forgiving of variations from the ideal, but their natural environment is temperature in the high 70s, pH 7.8 to 8.6, conductivity about 200 ìS.

The social structure of a community of *mbuna* is based on rock piles and aggression. The fish feed off the rocks, use the interstices as hiding places, and spawn in caves among the rocks. Males defend small territories around the boulders and court females there. Every cubic inch of the rock piles is prime real estate, and population density is extremely high. Aggression is intense, but short-lived—if a fish other than a ripe female enters a male's space, it is repelled violently, but the attack cuts off as soon as the boundary is reached. The most common method of controlling aggression in the aquarium is to keep a very large number of fish together in a very large tank. This way, aggression is diffused among many. Since victims of an attack cannot escape the confines of the aquarium, it is important that other fish distract the attacker before serious injury is inflicted. Because males also drive away females that are not ready to spawn, it is important to have a high female-to-male ratio as well.

Intentional overcrowding requires extra attention to filtration and water changes. For both, the idea is: the more, the better. For example, you can use an undergravel filter and a canister filter, or a couple of power filters and a canister. Water changes should be large, frequent, and regular.

In the aquarium the ideal *mbuna* setup is plenty of rocks, piled securely bottom to surface throughout most of the tank. To minimize weight on the bottom glass, lightweight, porous rocks like lava and tufa are often used. Rock dwellers are primarily vegetarian, scraping algae, *aufwuchs*, or both off the rocks. They should be fed an algae-based preparation, though they very much enjoy an occasional treat of frozen or freeze dried invertebrates, the same way they rapidly gobble up any tiny creature they expose in their foraging. There are many excellent choices on the market of vegetable-based cichlid foods. You can supplement with fresh or scalded vegetables such a squash slices, spinach, or peas squeezed out of their skins. Sexual dimorphism is typical, with males both larger and more colorful in most instances. Dummy egg spots on the male's anal fin appear to be more involved in mate selection than as originally thought in fooling the female into pecking at them to ensure she gets a mouthful of sperm to fertilize her eggs, though that benefit also certainly occurs.

Cyathochromis obliquidens
TREWAVAS 1935

7.6	7.8	8.0

Size: 6 inches (15 cm) TL.

Dietary Notes: A specialized feeder on algae, which it scrapes off plant leaves.

Remarks: Not often imported, this drab-for-Malawi cichlid is similar to the postulated ancestral haplochromine, resembling *Petrotilapia*. It is always found in shallow water, often among plants, off which it feeds. This is the only species in this genus.

Cynotilapia afra
(GÜNTHER 1894)

| 7.6 | 7.8 | 8.0 |

| 21.1 | 26.6 | 32.2 | 37.7 °C |
| 70 | 80 | 90 | 100 °F |

Trade names: red top afra, white top afra, yellow blaze afra, yellow bee, Mbamba black afra.

Size: 4 inches (10 cm) TL.

Dietary Notes: A plankton feeder.

Remarks: Widespread in the lake, populations from different areas are quite differently colored, and there are many morphs still to be assigned to a particular (or new) species. These are heralded as "dwarf mbuna," since they stay smaller than most. Some of the populations are especially beautifully colored. Males defend a cave in the rocks; females and non-breeding males feed in the water column.

Gephyrochromis lawsi
FRYER 1957

Size: 5 inches (13 cm) TL.

Dietary Notes: A sand sifter that feeds primarily on small invertebrates.

Remarks: This genus is normally found in deeper water, in sandy and intermediate habitats, alone or in small groups. It is found in the northern part of the lake.

Iodotropheus sprengerae
OLIVER & LOISELLE 1972

7.6	7.8	8.0

Trade Name: Rusty cichlid.

Size: 4.25 inches (11 cm) TL.

Dietary Notes: Generally herbivorous.

Remarks: One of the first cichlids imported from Malawi, this species, found at Boadzulu, Chinyankwazi, and Chinyamwezi Islands, is a perennial favorite. It is quite peaceful, doesn't dig up the tank, and breeds very readily. Males and females are colored alike. An excellent species for the beginning African enthusiast.

Iodotropheus stuartgranti
KONINGS 1990

7.6	7.8	8.0

Size: 4 inches (10 cm) TL.

Dietary Notes: More omnivorous than *I. sprengerae*.

Remarks: A dimorphic species, with blue males and silvery brown females. Also very peaceful. Found on the east coast north of the Nsinje River.

Labeotropheus fuelleborni
AHL 1926

| 7.6 | 7.8 | 8.0 |

Size: 6 inches (15 cm) TL.

Dietary Notes: Heavily herbivorous.

Remarks: This genus is easily recognized by its big nose and underslung mouth—adaptations for grazing algae. They graze from sediment-free rocks, leaving scrape marks. The fleshy nose serves as a fulcrum, and the fish is able to shear even tightly attached algae. Because they can feed on surfaces parallel to their body, they are able to graze in much shallower water than other cichlids, which orient themselves more perpendicular to the rocks when feeding. *L. fuelleborni* is deeper bodied than its close cousin *L. trewavasae*. Males are often intolerant of one another, so it is best to keep them either as a single specimen or in groups of one male to multiple females. Enormous variation in color patterns is observed in this fish, which is prevalent in the lake, and which has been popular in the hobby for a long time.

63

Labeotropheus trewavasae
FRYER 1956

| 7.6 | 7.8 | 8.0 |

Size: 6 inches (15 cm) TL.

Dietary Notes: Heavily herbivorous.

Remarks: This species, as well as *L. fuelleborni*, are easily distinguished from other Rift Lake cichlids by their blunt noses. *L. trewavasae* have a more elongated body when compared to *L. fuelleborni*, and when the two species are compared side by side, such differences in body shape are clear.

Labidochromis caeruleus
FRYER 1956

Trade names: Lemon cichlid, lemon drop cichlid, electric yellow lab

Size: 6 inches (13 cm) TL, females usually considerably smaller than males.

Dietary Notes: An omnivorous diet is best.

Remarks: Fish of this genus are peaceful for *mbuna*, and may not fare well with more aggressive species. In nature, this fish can be observed feeding off the ceilings of caves and deep within rock crevices. Aquarium specimens are not picky about the foods they consume, with most standard prepared foods being suitable. Round out their diet to include both plant and animal matter in equal quantities. Though named for a sky-blue morph, the intensely bright yellow morph, often with heavy black edges to its fins, is the one regularly seen. A common misconception is that only males have the black fins, but females can also be found with this coloration.

65

Labidochromis chisumlae
FRYER 1956

Size: 4 inches (10 cm) TL.

Behavior: Generally peaceful.

Dietary Notes: Omnivorous.

Remarks: *Labidochromis chisumulae* is found in many different habitats, but is always associated with rocks (Konings 1990). They are not quite as common as *L. caeruleus*, but many cichlid specialists have access to broodstock or sometimes even wild stock. Their care and husbandry is identical to that of *L. caeruleus*.

***Labidochromis* sp. "perlmutt"**

Size: 4 inches (10 cm) TL.

Dietary Notes: Omnivorous.

Remarks: This yet undescribed fish, named (in German) for its mother-of-pearl coloration, is similar to *L. caeruleus*, of which it may be a geographical variant. It is easy to breed and keep, like all its congeners, and is quite popular due to its unusual coloration.

Labidochromis zebroides
LEWIS 1982

Size: 4 inches (10 cm) TL.

Dietary Notes: Omnivorous.

Remarks: Until recently, this species had not been exported in significant numbers, and compared to others in the genus, they still aren't. However, they are quite a bit more common today than they were years ago, and though captive-bred specimens are hard to come by, a little wait will be well worth it. Their care and husbandry in aquariums is identical to that of others in the genus.

Melanochromis auratus
(BOULENGER 1897)

| 7.6 | 7.8 | 8.0 |

Size: 5 inches (12 cm) TL.

Dietary Notes: Omnivorous, but should have a high-vegetable diet.

Remarks: This genus is well established in the hobby, and this species has been a favorite for years. Its marked sexual dimorphism, in which males and females seem to be negative images of each other, is one of its attractions. This is often an extremely aggressive species, and the author has had entire tanks wiped out by an intolerant male. Such a fish will take on other cichlids many times its size…and win! The color pattern of this cichlid remains identical throughout their range, but the intensity of the yellow in the females and the brown in the males varies among populations (Konings 1990). Konings further reports that the most intensely colored individuals are found around Mbenji, Maleri, and Mumbo Islands.

69

Melanochromis chipokae
JOHNSON 1975

Size: 5 inches (12 cm) TL.

Dietary Notes: An opportunistic micropredator, often of cichlid fry.

Remarks: *M. chipokae* is characterized by its large size and lively coloration (Konings 1990). Their care in aquariums is identical to others in the genus, with no special exceptions. Use caution when adding this fish to cichlid community aquariums, as they tend to be outwardly aggressive, even to fishes they would never be able to swallow.

Melanochromis dialeptos
BOWERS & STAUFFER, 1997

7.6	7.8	8.0

Trade Name: Dwarf auratus.

Size: 3 inches (8 cm) TL.

Dietary Notes: Omnivorous.

Remarks: This fish was prevalent in the hobby due to its novelty as a "dwarf" *mbuna*, but it has lost some popularity recently. It is very much like an *M. auratus* on a smaller scale.

Melanochromis johannii
(ECCLES 1973)

Trade Name: Electric blue.

Size: 5 inches (12 cm) TL.

Dietary Notes: Omnivorous.

Remarks: This species has a dark blue and black breeding
male with juveniles, females, and non breeding males being
bright orange. A single-species tank, therefore, makes a
stunningly contrastive display. The literature on this species
is divided; some say it is the least aggressive of the genus,
while others find the opposite. My experience with this fish
is that it is one of the most aggressive mbuna, though not
quite as bad as *M. auratus*.

Melanochromis labrosus
(Trewavas 1935)

7.6	7.8	8.0

21.1 26.6 32.2 37.7 °C
70 80 90 100 °F

Size: 4 inches (10 cm) TL.

Dietary Notes: Feeds primarily in horizontal fissures in the rocks on small fish and aufwuchs.

Remarks: Though it remains in this genus, this fish is quite different from its congeners. It is highly laterally compressed, a feature which, like its enlarged, fleshy lips, is an adaptation to feeding in cracks and crevices where other fish cannot reach. A cryptic species, it is rare in the hobby and is infrequently encountered in the lake, though studies with rotenone demonstrate that it is more numerous than direct observations would indicate.

Metriaclima aurora
(Burgess 1976)
Size: 5 inches (12 cm) TL.

Metriaclima barlowi
(McKaye & Staiffer 1986)
Size: 5 inches (12 cm) TL.

Metriaclima callainos
Stauffer, Bowers, Kellogg, &
McKaye 1997
Size: 5 inches (12 cm) TL.

Metriaclima estherae
(Konings 1995)
Size: 5 inches (12 cm) TL.

Metriaclima greshakei
(Meyer & Foerster 1984)
Size: 5 inches (12 cm) TL.

Metriaclima hajomaylandi
(Myer & Schartl 1984)
Size: 5 inches (12 cm) TL.

Please see remarks opposite
regarding care and husbandry.

Metriaclima livingstoni
(BOULENGE 1899)

7.6	7.8	8.0

Size: 5" (12 cm) TL.

Dietary Notes: An algae and aufwuchs feeder.

Remarks: In nature, non-breeding individuals are commonly encountered over sandy areas. Juveniles take refuge in snail shells and have distinctively striped caudal fins. They often live commensally with a species of catfish within the shell. Of course, females holding eggs or young will be well-hidden deep within the recesses of the boulders in the lake. In aquariums, this species is distinctive, but never seems to get the attention we think it deserves. Those of you looking for something interesting for your Rift Lake tank may want to consider this fish.

Region 2 • Lake Malawi

Metriaclima lanisticola
(Burgess 1976)
Size: 5 inches (12 cm) TL.

Metriaclima lombardoi
(Burgess 1971)
Size: 5 inches (12 cm) TL.

Metriaclima mbenjii
(Stauffer, Bowers, Kellogg, &
McKaye 1997)
Size: 5 inches (12 cm) TL.

Metriaclima zebra "Albino"
(Boulenger 1899)
Size: 5 inches (12 cm) TL.

Metriaclima zebra "OB"
(Boulenger 1899)
Size: 5 inches (12 cm) TL.

Metriaclima callainos "Pearl"
Stauffer, Bowers, Kellogg, &
McKaye 1997
Size: 5 inches (12 cm) TL.

Please see remarks opposite
regarding care and husbandry.

Metriaclima zebra
(BOULENGER 1899)

7.6	7.8	8.0

Size: 5 inches (12 cm) TL.

Dietary Notes: An algae and aufwuchs feeder.

Remarks: Malawi zebras are often referred to as the original mbuna. Many years ago, when we first saw shipments of this species, they were mixed with many other mbuna from various regions. At that time, they were all lumped into one genus (*Pseudotropheus*) and a single species (*zebra*). Today, tireless efforts by several notable ichthyologists have split this genus into many genera with many more species.

Petrotilapia chrysos
STAUFFER & SWIK 1996

| 7.6 | 7.8 | 8.0 |

Size: 5 inches (13 cm) TL, females usually considerably smaller than males.

Dietary Notes: Combs diatoms from filamentous algae and feeds on plankton.

Remarks: This species is found in the southeast part of the lake, at Chinyankwazi and Chinyamwezi islands. This genus is considered more primitive, or less derived, than most *mbuna*, similar to the open-water cichlids in the lake. It has adapted to a peculiar trophic niche, feeding off the aufwuchs on the algae, leaving behind bare filaments, which other cichlids eat.

Petrotilapia tridentiger
TREWAVAS 1935

| 7.6 | 7.8 | 8.0 |

Size: 6 inches (15 cm) TL; possibly larger in aquaria.

Dietary Notes: Combs diatoms from filamentous algae and feeds on plankton.

Remarks: Widespread in rocky zones throughout the lake. Like all *Petrotilapia* species, *tridentiger* use their tricuspid teeth and large mouth to feed from the sediment-free biocover on rocks in their native habitat (Konings 1990). In aquariums, this species may become very aggressive during breeding, so be sure to keep a careful eye on them in cichlid community aquariums.

***Pseudotropheus* sp. "acei"**
Undescribed to date
Size: 5 inches (12 cm) TL.

Pseudotropheus demasoni
Konings 1994
Size: 3 inches (8 cm) TL.

Pseudotropheus elongatus
Fryer 1976
Size: 6 inches (15 cm) TL.

Pseudotropheus saulosi
Konings 1990
Size: 3 inches (7.5 cm) TL.

***Pseudotropheus* sp.**
Undescribed to date
Size: 5 inches (12 cm) TL.

***Pseudotropheus* sp. "Albino"**
Size: 5 inches (12 cm) TL.

Please see remarks opposite
regarding care and husbandry.

Pseudotropheus crabro
(Ribbink & Lewis 1982)

7.6	7.8	8.0

Trade Names: Bumblebee or hornet cichlid.

Size: 6 inches (15 cm) TL.

Dietary Notes: An algae and aufwuchs feeder.

Remarks: This species is especially known for growing larger in captivity than in the wild; some specimens have reached 8 inches (20 cm). It enjoys an unusual symbiosis with the catfish *Bagrus meriodionalis*. It serves as a cleaner, removing ectoparasites from the catfish, which can grow to a length of 4 feet, but it also feeds on the eggs of the catfish. Apparently, it changes color to a dull brown when it raids the nests so that the parents do not see the familiar striped fish eating their spawn.

Pseudotropheus socolofi
Johnson 1974

| 7.6 | 7.8 | 8.0 |

Size: 5 inches (12 cm) TL.

Dietary Notes: An algae and aufwuchs feeder.

Remarks: Extremely popular for its light blue color, *P. socolofi* is found in populations that have a dark edge to the dorsal fin and populations without the black band. Additionally, their heads are broad and rounded, giving them a bullish appearance. They are aggressive, but less so than many other *mbuna*. An domesticated albino form has become popular.

Tropheops tropheops
(REGAN 1922)

Size: 7 inches (17.5 cm) TL.

Dietary Notes: An algae and plankton feeder.

Remarks: Here is another complex of populations that will probably resolve into several species, though highly variable ones, still. They feed at an angle of about 45°, ripping strands of algae from the rocks. Like *M. livingstoni*, this species is not as popular as it should be, because of their hardiness in aquaria, and like *P. crabro* and *M. lombardoi*, they can grow larger than what has been published about them previously.

Open Water Haps

The open-water Malawi species live most or all of their lives outside the rocky zones. Even when found in rocky areas, they are there to feed on the *mbuna*, not to associate with the rocky habitat itself. As a result, the level of aggression they display is considerably less than that of *mbuna*. Coupled with the different dietary requirements of these two groups, this makes it unwise to attempt a community containing both types.

Natural History & Captive Husbandry

Proper water conditions, of course, are the same for these cichlids as for *mbuna*. The aquarium, however, should not be filled with rocks, since these fish need open swimming room. Providing caves and crevices for hiding spots is still a good idea, but you don't need the reef look of *mbuna* tanks. They are

generally large fishes—ranging from 8 inches (20 cm) to 14 inches (35 cm)—and require very large tanks.

The male of these species typically takes on a vibrant mating coloration, while juveniles, females, and non breeding males are drabber. In an aquarium only the dominant male(s) will be in color. Although there are exceptions, most of the non-peacock open-water cichlids are silvery brown, with the males having blue nuptial coloration. A dark stripe, either horizontal or oblique, is a common feature as well. Also common are species that have three dark spots on their sides.

Open water species are typically planktonivores, insectivores, or piscivores. They will be very happy if you feed them live foods such as they eat in the wild, but they will thrive nicely on any commercial cichlid pellet. Flake food can be used, but it shouldn't form the basis of the diet, as it is not substantial enough for large animals in most cases. The larger piscivores can be easily maintained on large meaty foods such as pieces of fish, shrimp, krill, and pellets or sticks.

TAXONOMY

In the quagmire of Malawi cichlid taxonomy, there is a great deal of disagreement, and, as with the rock dwelling cichlids, the open-water species are constantly being revised. Although we are far from the original situation in which almost all species were assigned to the genus *Haplochromis*, there are currently a large number of monotypic genera, as well as three remaining catchall groups. Leftover obliquely striped species are in *Mylochromis*, three-spotted species are in *Otopharynx*, and barred species are in *Placidochromis*. It is clear that further revision will be made.

Aristochromis christyi
TREWAVAS 1935

Size: 12 inches (30 cm) TL.

Dietary Notes: A voracious piscivore that will take almost any prepared food greedily.

Remarks: This cichlid feeds on mbuna in the wild, turning on its side and slurping them out of crevices. It needs a very large tank—upwards of 200 gallons. The only species in the genus, this fish's most notable feature is its inchesaristocratic inches nose. The black stripe from the top of the head to the tail disappears when the male is in his blue breeding color.

Aulonocara baenschi
MEYER & RIEHL 1985

Trade Names: Yellow Peacock

Size: 6 inches (15 cm) TL.

Dietary Notes: Eats primarily invertebrates in the wild.

Remarks: Bright yellow fishes are rare in freshwater aquariums, but luckily we have this species available to us. They are easily cared for, provided that their diet consists of both plant and animal matter. Breeding males of this genus, the peacock cichlids, are brilliantly and variably colored. Domestic strains are often hybridized, and it seems as if every farm produces its own unique variety. This is unfortunate, since the natural species and races are profoundly beautiful.

87

Aulonocara ethelwynnae
Meyer, Riehl & Zetzsche 1987
Size: 4 inches (10 cm) TL.

Aulonocara hansbaenschi
Meyer, Riehl & Zetzsche 1987
Size: 6 inches (15 cm) TL.

Aulonocara hueseri
Meyer, Riehl & Zetzsche 1987
Size: 4 inches (10 cm) TL.

Aulonocara jacobfreibergi
Meyer, Riehl & Zetzsche 1987
Size: 6 inches (5 cm) TL.

Aulonocara maylandi
Trewavas 1984
Size: 4 inches (10 cm) TL.

Aulonocara saulosi
Meyer, Riehl & Zetzsche 1987
Size: 6 inches (15 cm) TL.

> Please see remarks opposite
> for additional information.

Aulonocara steveni
MEYER, RIEHL & ZETZSCHE 1987

Size: 6 inches (15 cm) TL.

Dietary Notes: Eats primarily invertebrates in the wild.

Remarks: Aulonocara steveni are easily recognized by the light blue stripe that travels along the dorsal edge. Additionally, they have a nearly-solid-yellow-to-rusty flank and metallic blue head.

Aulonocara stuartgranti
MEYER & RIEHL 1985

Size: 6 inches (15 cm) TL.

Dietary Notes: Eats primarily invertebrates in the wild.

Remarks: Here is another cichlid that has multiple color variations. Each color morph may have a different name, giving the impression of being multiple species or subspecies.

Buccochromis lepturus
(REGAN 1922)

Size: 17 inches (42 cm) TL.

Dietary Notes: A piscivore.

Remarks: *B. lepturus* is a predator that hunts over sandy or rubble areas in Lake Malawi. Not much is known about their breeding in aquariums. It is thought that pairs nest in the open or in close proximity to rocky outcroppings. Provide a large aquarium for this robust cichlid.

Buccochromis rhoadesii
BOULENGER 1908

Size: 14 inches (35 cm) TL.

Dietary Notes: Piscivorous.

Remarks: This species hunts fishes in the open sandy areas of Lake Malawi. Their care and husbandry in aquariums is generally the same as other large predatory cichlids, with good filtration, high-quality foods, a very large aquarium, and frequent water changes being the most important aspects.

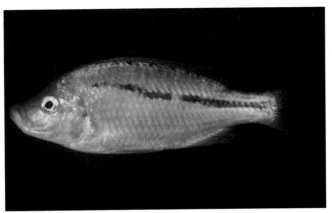

Caprichromis orthognathus
(TREWAVAS 1935)

Size: 8 inches (20 cm) TL.

Dietary Notes: A pedophage.

Remarks: One of the most interesting cichlids in the lake, both morphologically and behaviorally. This and its congener, *C. liemi,* are specifically adapted to feed on the eggs and larvae of other cichlids. The nearly-vertical mouth and flat head are used in its peculiar feeding strategy—the fish rams holding female cichlids from below, causing them to eject their brood, which is then gobbled up. This species has a typical haplochromine oblique black stripe, which it displays or not, depending on the coloration of its intended prey (Oliver). Stomach content analysis of these fish reveals only eggs, larvae, and fry.

Champsochromis caeruleus
(BOULENGER 1908)

  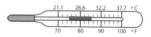

Trade Names: Malawi trout, trout cichlid, Haplochromis thola.

Size: 13 inches (33 cm) TL.

Dietary Notes: A piscivore.

Remarks: One look at this fish and you can see that it is a pursuit predator. Its streamlined body is enhanced by long, flowing finnage, especially in adult males. A huge aquarium is necessary to enjoy this species in captivity. This species is similar to its only congener, *C. spilorhynchus.*

Cheilochromis euchilus
(TREWAVAS 1935)

Size: 14 inches (35 cm) TL.

Dietary Notes: Insectivorous.

Remarks: Monotypic. Adults develop large, fleshy lips. Such adaptations permit the fish to seal crevices and suck out the prey within—in this case aquatic insects. Juveniles lack this feature. It should be noted here that a group of Middle American cichlids, of the genus *Amphilophus,* also exhibits this unique trait.

Chilotilapia rhoadesii
(BOULENGER 1908)

Trade Names: Road's cichlid.
Size: 10 inches (25 cm) TL.
Dietary Notes: Eats principally snails in the wild.
Remarks: Another monotypic genus. *Cheilochromis euchilus* was at one time classified as *Chilotilapia euchilus*, and *C. rhoadesii* is barely distinguishable from that species. Both species do well in large aquariums with other peaceful fishes of equal size and temperament. This cichlid has powerful jaws for crushing snail shells.

Copadichromis chrysonotus
(BOULENGER 1908)

| 7.6 | 7.8 | 8.0 |

Size: 6 inches (15 cm) TL.

Dietary Notes: A planktonivore.

Remarks: *C. chrysonotus* live in the open water of sheltered bays, where they are commonly found over rocks. The rocks can be some distance below them, with depths of over 35 feet (10 meters) not being uncommon. They can be identified by three large, black spots on the flanks. Of course, several other species have this type of pattern, but *C. chrysonotus* are more commonly available. Therefore, if your specimen has such features, it has a good chance of being this species.

Copadichromis cyaneus
(TREWAVAS 1935)

Size: 6 inches (15 cm) TL.

Dietary Notes: A planktonivore.

Remarks: Unlike their congeners, *C. cyaneus* is only found in clear water over sediment-free rocks. Otherwise, their care and husbandry in aquariums is identical to others in the group.

Copadichromis jacksoni
(Iles 1960)

Size: 8 inches (20 cm) TL.

Dietary Notes: A planktonivore.

Remarks: Large schools of *C. jacksoni* can be observed in the deeper waters of sheltered bays throughout the lake. They are commonly associated with aufwuchs-covered rocks. Unlike other *Copadichromis*, this species prefers slightly darker aquariums.

99

Copadichromis mloto
(Iles 1960)

Size: 8 inches (20 cm) TL.

Dietary Notes: A planktonivore.

Remarks: In nature, you can find *C. mloto* over sandy bottoms in shallow water. Under actinic lighting, this species—as well as many others from Lake Malawi—seems to fluoresce a deep, metallic blue color. They are stunning fish that do well with other species of similar size and behavior.

Copadichromis pleurostigma
(Trewavas 1935)

  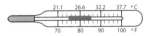

Size: 6 inches (15 cm) TL.

Dietary Notes: A planktonivore.

Remarks: Not too long ago this species was impossible to obtain, with the only exceptions being those specimens that came in either as special orders, those that were collected by hobbyists visiting the lake, or in mixed bags of miscellaneous cichlids. Today, we enjoy the rarity of this species, but thankfully, they are more commonly available than they used to be.

Cyrtocara moorii
BOULENGER 1902

Trade Names: Blue dolphin.

Size: 8 inches (20 cm) TL.

Dietary Notes: This species follows large cichlids like *Taeniolethrinops* and feeds on invertebrates dug up by them.

Remarks: This species is one of the most easily identifiable cichlids of Lake Malawi. They resemble a solid blue frontosa with their large, pronounced nuchal hump. Their care and husbandry in aquariums is similar to that of the closely related *Copadichromis* species.

Dimidiochromis compressiceps

Boulenger 1908

Trade Names: Malawi eye biter.

Size: 10 inches (25 cm) TL.

Dietary Notes: A piscivore.

Remarks: This fish earned its nickname of incheseye-biter inches due to their alleged behavior of plucking the eyes out of tankmates. Although there are some conflicting reports, it is unlikely that this nickname has any validity. Loss of an eye in cichlid aggression is not uncommon in captivity, and in such a case it makes no sense to pin this reputation on an entire species. In the wild it is found in grassy habitats, where it is an ambush predator of schooling juvenile cichlids.

Exochochromis anagenys
OLIVER 1989

Trade Name: Malawi torpedo.

Size: 12 inches (30 cm) TL.

Dietary Notes: A piscivore.

Remarks: This species is the only one in its genus. A streamlined cichlid, it feeds on small fish in the rocky shallows. In aquariums, they are fairly rambunctious and often damage their snouts by constantly rubbing them on the glass.

Fossorochromis rostratus

(Boulenger 1899)

  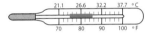

Size: 10 inches (25 cm) TL.

Dietary Notes: Feeds on invertebrates.

Remarks: Another monotypic genus. This species is widespread in the lake in shallow sandy areas, where it feeds on insects and small crustaceans.

105

Nimbochromis fuscotaeniatus
(Regan 1922)
Size: 10 inches (25 cm) TL.

Nimbochromis linni
(Burgess & Axelrod 1975)
Size: 10 inches (25 cm) TL.

Nimbochromis livingstoni
(Günther 1894)
Size: 10 inches (25 cm) TL.

Nimbochromis livingstoni
(Günther 1894)
Size: 10 inches (25 cm) TL.

Nimbochromis venustus
(Boulenger 1908)
Size: 10 inches (25 cm) TL.

Nimbochromis venustus
(Boulenger 1908)
Size: 10 inches (25 cm) TL.

Please see remarks opposite
for additional information.

Nimbochromis polystigma
(REGAN 1922)

Size: 9 inches (23 cm) TL.
Dietary Notes: Piscivore.
Remarks: *N. polystigma* is a predator that hunts its prey in several ways. Sometimes, single specimens can be observed actually chasing small fishes throughout weed beds, but they have also been observed hunting in a similar fashion to *N. livingstoni*. Regardless, they are an effective predator, and such efficiency does not end in the wild. Captive specimens will make short work of fishes they can swallow in your aquarium, too.

Otopharynx heterodon
TREWAVAS 1935

| 7.6 | 7.8 | 8.0 |

Size: 6 inches (15 cm) TL.

Dietary Notes: Omnivore.

Remarks: *O. heterodon* is a rather small cichlid that will not usually be confused with others. Juveniles exhibit three small blotches along the flanks. Additionally, this species is more deep-bodied than others of the genus.

Otopharynx lithobates
OLIVER 1989

Size: 6 inches (15 cm) TL.

Dietary Notes: A copraphage.

Remarks: It might come as a surprise to many hobbyists already familiar with the outstanding appearance of this species that it is in fact a cave dweller. Rarely are *O. lithobates* in breeding dress observed outside their secluded hideaways. They scavenge the sediment in caves and feed on the droppings of other fish, mainly herbivorous species.

Placidochromis electra
(Burgess 1979)

| 7.6 | 7.8 | 8.0 |

Size: 6 inches (15 cm) TL.

Dietary Notes: Follows large cichlids that stir up the sandy bottom, opportunistically feeding on invertebrates exposed by the digging.

Remarks: This is not usually a shy fish, and they are frequently found over sandy substrates. While they are routinely observed also in shallow waters, *P. electra* was initially collected at a depth greater than 48 feet (15 meters), giving rise to its common name of deep water hap.

Placidochromis milomo
OLIVER 1989

| 7.6 | 7.8 | 8.0 |

21.1   26.6   32.2   37.7 °C
70   80   90   100 °F

Trade Names: Super VC-10

Size: 8 inches (20 cm) TL.

Dietary Notes: A predator.

Remarks: The VC-10 is distributed lakewide. They exhibit a unique coloration that is quite difficult to confuse with any other species in the lake. Feeding consists of pressing their fleshy lips, which act as a plunger, over small holes or crevices that contain shrimps or other invertebrates and then sucking the animals out whole.

Protomelas fenestratus
(TREWAVAS 1935)

7.6	7.8	8.0

Size: 8 inches (20 cm) TL.

Dietary Notes: Feeds by blowing sediment off rocks and picking up whatever is underneath.

Remarks: Unless the locality is known, *P. fenestratus* is quite difficult to distinguish from its close cousin *P. taeniolatus*. The race with the largest individuals is reported to occur at Taiwan Reef, and this is the same locality in which many specimens in the aquarium industry originally came from. Their care and husbandry in captivity is very basic, and as long as they are provided with good quality water and a large aquarium, they will do very well for many years.

Protomelas similis
(REGAN 1922)

Size: 6 inches (15 cm) TL.

Dietary Notes: Largely herbivorous.

Remarks: Found mainly in shallow areas that are heavily vegetated. Konings reports that they are abundant in some places but completely absent in others. Males will use their sharp teeth to crop the weeds just above the sand's surface. Here a nest will be made and a female will be tempted into spawning with him. After spawning, the mouthbrooding females move into deep cover within the weeds while the male lures in another mate.

Protomelas taeniolatus
(TREWAVAS 1935)

Size: 6 inches (15 cm) TL.

Dietary Notes: Feeds on aufwuchs and plankton.

Remarks: It has been suggested that this species contains many races because they are restricted to rocky habitats. Otherwise, *P. taeniolatus* is easy to keep and breed in aquariums that are set up to allow them enough room to practice their ritualistic courtship.

Rhamphochromis ferox
REGAN 1922

| 7.6 | 7.8 | 8.0 |

Size: 18 inches (45 cm) TL.

Dietary Notes: A piscivore.

Remarks: This awesome open-water-roaming predatory cichlid is probably the closest thing to a barracuda you could find—unless you're an *Acestrorhynchus* fan, of course. They need very, very large aquariums with extremely clean water and strong filtration in order to thrive for extended periods in captivity.

Rhamphochromis macrophthalmus
REGAN 1922

Size: 12 inches (30 cm) TL.

Dietary Notes: A piscivore.

Remarks: Of all the species in *Rhamphochromis*, this one is the only species that you may see with any regularity. They are big—albeit not quite as big as the others, but they still need very large aquarium with good, strong filtration. They are easily identified by their yellowish-orange ventral fins and anal fin.

Rhamphochromis woodi
REGAN 1922

Size: 18 inches (45 cm) TL.

Dietary Notes: A piscivore.

Remarks: Perhaps the least common of the sometimes-available species within the genus is this species. They only surefire way to tell them apart from the others is the lack of the lateral stripe that is commonly seen in *R. macrophthalmus*. Additionally, the head of *R. woodi* is very large and measures less than three times of the fish's overall standard length. In some specimens, the mouth protrudes noticeably more than it does in other species.

Sciaenochromis ahli
(Trewavas 1935)

Size: 6 inches (15 cm) TL.

Dietary Notes: A piscivore, eating fry and juvenile cichlids.

Remarks: Apparently, this is *not* the fish commonly known as inches*S. ahli.* inches Konings in 1993 compared the fish known in the trade by that name with the holotype and determined that they were not the same. Thus, the species long known by this name is actually *S. fryeri.* The fish in this genus are mild for Malawi cichlids and should be kept with similarly peaceful species.

Sciaenochromis fryeri

Konings 1993

Trade Names: Electric blue, electric blue inchesahli, inches icecap electric blue.

Size: 6 inches (15 cm) TL.

Dietary Notes: A piscivore, eating fry and juvenile cichlids.

Remarks: By any name this cichlid is gorgeous. The male breeding dress is a vivid bright blue. Some of the geographical variants have a white blaze from the nose down the back. An old, widespread, but uncommon cichlid in the lake, this fish is extremely common in the hobby. It's easy breeding and large broods (up to 70 fry) contribute greatly to its prevalence.

Stigmatochromis woodi
(REGAN 1922)

Size: 10 inches (25 cm) TL.

Dietary Notes: A piscivore.

Remarks: A typical three-spot predator, this is the type species for its genus. There are many different races of this large cichlid found throughout the lake. Some are said to have smaller mouths, while others have better coloration. This species is not common in the aquarium trade.

Tyrannochromis macrostoma (nigriventer)
(REGAN 1922)

7.6	7.8	8.0

Size: 14 inches (35 cm) TL.

Dietary Notes: An ambush predator.

Remarks: There is a great deal of confusion about this genus, first whether there are two or four species. Then it isn't clear if the species usually found in the trade is macrostoma or nigriventer. Even these names indicate there may have been some confusion originally, since nigriventer (black belly) is reported to have a lighter belly than macrostoma. In any case, with a well-chosen name that translates roughly as incheslarge-mouthed terrible cichlid, inches this is clearly a fish that small mbuna should fear. They have been found with cichlids a couple of inches long in their stomachs.

Chapter 5

Region 3
Lake
Tanganyika

Lake Tanganyika is a very large, very old, and very deep lake. In fact, it is almost a mile deep at its deepest but due to its extremely stable water parameters, which prevent complete thermal mixing and lake turnover, only the top few hundred feet contain sufficient oxygen to support fish life. There is speculation that geothermal heating in its depths may account for Tanganyika's lack of much of a thermocline, but whatever the cause, the lake is extremely stable both in temperature and in chemistry.

These parameters, which aquarists should try to mimic in their tanks, are:

Temperature within a degree or two of 80°F (27°C), pH average 9, sometimes even higher, conductivity at least 600 ppm, and very high alkalinity. The latter is extremely important, as the lake water is highly buffered and stable. Since most metabolic processes produce acid, the alkalinity of the water in an aquarium can quickly become depleted, resulting in a pH drop.

There has been much hypothesizing about the relationships of these cichlids to each other and to other African species, with opposing views of this ancient lake as a reservoir of archaic cichlid lineages or as an evolutionary hotspot from which other

African lineages derive. DNA studies are beginning to shed light on the phylogeny of these cichlids. A comprehensive study has shown that both views are supported by the data (Salzburger, Meyer, Baric, Verheyen, & Sturmbauer), as they found evidence of both ancestral cichlid lineages in the lake and radiation throughout Africa as a result of the rise of the Haplochromini in the lake. It is obvious that further studies are needed, which should provide more details about this fascinating group of species.

The great diversity of behaviors, including reproductive strategies, among Tanganyika cichlids makes it preferable to discuss natural history husbandry for each group, rather than for the flock as a whole as we did for Malawi cichlids.

TILAPIINES

Aside from being polyphyletic, the tilapiines are a very diverse group, with substrate spawners, biparental mouthbrooders, and maternal mouthbrooders. The two Tanganyikan fish assigned to this group underscore this diversity. Though the one dwarfs the other, both are very large fish. The mouthbrooder is a typical tilapiine, being a detritus feeder, while the substrate spawner is a pursuit predator.

Natural History and Captive Husbandry

Huge aquaria, massive filtration, and copious water changes are the key to successful maintenance. The diet of *Oreochromis* should be heavily vegetarian, while that of *Boulengerochromis* should reflect its piscivorous nature.

Boulengerochromis microlepis
(BOULENGER 1899)

Size: 40 inches (100 cm).

Dietary Notes: A piscivore.

Remarks: This fish is in a monotypic genus, and some would put it in its own tribe, too: Boulengerochromini (Takahsi). It is the world's largest cichlid—the Tanganyikan "shark." Although it has been bred in captivity, there are still a lot of unanswered questions about its breeding behavior. The spawns are extremely large—10,000—and the fry are extremely small, said to require plankton before growing large enough for baby brine shrimp. The parents apparently do not eat when breeding, and, since they guard the fry until they are very large, the adults are believed to die after a once-in-a-lifetime spawning. It is known that if the fry are removed, the pair will resume eating and then spawn again in captivity.

Oreochromis tanganicae
(GÜNTHER 1894)

Size: 16.5 inches (42 cm).

Dietary Notes: In the wild it feeds mainly on diatoms.

Remarks: A large fish requiring very large tanks. They can be quite aggressive with conspecifics, but they usually ignore other species. This is a maternal mouthbrooder.

LAMPROLOGINES

A highly divergent group of cichlids, the lamprologines of Tanganyika maintain a major ecological presence in an environment very much like that of the *mbuna* in Lake Malawi. In that group, herbivorous maternal mouthbreeders live aggressive, territorial lives, with their agonistic behavior directed mainly at conspecifics entering their spawning/feeding territories. The lamps, on the other hand, are mostly micropredators and planktonivores, and they tend their eggs in caves and crevices. Although they defend their territories vigorously to protect their fry, it is mainly from predators, and, depending on species, conspecifics may share the care of the fry.

Natural History and Captive Husbandry

Since pair bonding is strong in many of the monogamous species, the best way to obtain a breeding pair is to raise a group of juveniles together, removing fish that get picked on until just a pair remains. Polygamous shelldwellers can be kept in colonies, though with some species even in very large tanks it may be impossible to keep more than one male.

These fish can be kept and bred in large community tanks, but the strategy for maintaining such groupings is markedly different from that for *mbuna*. Plenty of rockwork is again in order, but rather than overcrowding them to diffuse aggression, you must provide enough room for each pair to have its own territory.

Water quality is extremely important and should be maintained through regular water changes. Although many aquarists recommend avoiding large water changes with Tanganyikans, my experience with them has been the same as with all other fish—the more the merrier thrive. The key is water stability; if you make regular large changes, the water does not have time to deteriorate.

A Special Taxonomic Note

A special taxonomic note is in order concerning the lamprologines. *"Lamprologus"* was a catchall genus, and the first split noticed by hobbyists was the erection of the genus *Neolamprologus*, which took in many of the lamps in Lake Tanganyika. This split was predicated on the fact that the type species is the riverine *L. congoensis*. Unfortunately it left confusion of what to do with the others. Some aquarists made the bold (and erroneous) assumption that all Tanganyikan species once assigned to *Lamprologus* were now in *Neolamprologus*, while others assumed the names were interchangeable—as reflected in the number of dealer lists which label all the species *"Lamprologus/Neolamprologus."* Things were further confused by the rise in availability of various shelldwellers that came in labeled correctly as *Neolamprologus* at this time, which led to the reasonable but incorrect assumption that shelldwellers were *Neolamprologus*, while larger species were *Lamprologus*.

Here we will follow the use of *Neolamprologus* for congeners of the type species, *N. tetracanthus*. We recognize that the remaining *Lamprologus* almost certainly will be subject to further revision, and, with more than 50 species, even *Neolamprologus* may be split later on. If you do not find the fish you're seeking under one of these genera, try under the other.

Altolamprologus calvus
(POLL 1978)

Trade Names: Black calvus, white calvus, pearly calvus, calvus.

Size: 6 inches (15 cm) TL.

Dietary Notes: A micropredator.

Remarks: The two fish in this genus ("tall lamprologus") represent a real departure from the general fusiform shape of most larger lamps, and they also vary greatly from population to population, giving rise to a range of color/location names to distinguish them. All of these fish show an exaggerated degree of lateral compression, which enables them to live in cracks and crevices in their native habitat and feed on aquatic invertebrates as well as cichlid fry, which they can follow into fissures. A female often chooses an opening for a spawning site that is too small to admit the larger male. In such a case, the male spreads his milt outside the crevice, and when the female exits, water rushes in, bringing the sperm into contact with the eggs.

129

Altolamprologus compressiceps
(BOULENGER 1898)

| 7.8 | 8.0 | + |

Trade Names: Compressiceps, black compressiceps, white compressiceps, gold head, red fin compressiceps.

Size: 6 inches (15 cm) TL.

Dietary Notes: A micropredator.

Remarks: Another cichlid species that exhibits a high degree of lateral compression and great variety of population types. Like its congener, this is a relatively peaceful fish, at least toward other species, and is generally safe with any fish too large to ingest. Neither of the fish in this genus does well competing for food with more aggressive cichlids.

Chalinochromis brichardi
POLL 1974

Trade Names: Masked cichlid.

Size: 5 inches (12 cm) TL.

Dietary Notes: A micropredator.

Remarks: This genus contains fish with torpedo-shaped bodies much like *Julidochromis*. They live and breed among the rocks and rubble. This species is marked with black on the head and face, while the next two have black lines on the body as well.

Chalinochromis sp. "ndobhoi"
Size: 5 inches (12 cm) TL.

Size: 5 inches (12 cm) TL.
Dietary Notes: A micropredator.
Remarks: This yet-undescribed species has become established in the hobby. Looking a bit like a *C. popelini* whose stripes are turned to dashes (which is actually a retention of juvenile *Chalinochromis* coloration), it is a typical rock dweller with a fondness for tiny crustaceans like baby brine shrimp.

Chalinochromis popelini
BRICHARD 1989

| 7.8 | 8.0 | + |

21.1 26.6 32.2 37.7 °C
70 80 90 100 °F

Size: 6 inches (15 cm) TL.

Dietary Notes: A micropredator.

Remarks: Marked with black lines much like a *Julidichromis*, this species is a great choice for the rock zone of a Tanganyikan setup.

Julidochromis marlieri
Poll 1956
Size: 5 inches (13 cm) TL.

Julidochromis ornatus
Boulenger 1898
Size: 3.5 inches (8.5 cm) TL.

Julidochromis regani
Poll 1942
Size: 5 inches (13 cm) TL.

Julidochromis transcriptus
Matthes 1959
Size: 3 inches (7.5 cm) TL.

Julidochromis ornatus
Boulenger 1898
Size: 3.5 inches (8.5 cm) TL.

Julidochromis regani
Poll 1942
Size: 5 inches (13 cm) TL.

Please see remarks opposite
regarding care and husbandry.

Julidochromis dickfeldi
STAECK 1975

Size: 4 inches (10 cm) TL.

Dietary Notes: A micropredator.

Remarks: *Julidochromis* are best kept in pairs in medium-sized aquariums where they can breed among the rocks. Be sure to provide many caves and crevices. Like all fish in this genus, these fascinating fish seem almost tethered to their rock, they orient with their belly toward the rock no matter what position they take, always ready to zip back into a crevice. This species is blue and black, while its congeners often show a lot of yellow.

135

Lamprologus callipterus
BOULENGER 1906

| 7.8 | 8.0 | + |

Size: 6 inches (15 cm) TL for males, 1.75 inches (4.5 cm) TL females.

Dietary Notes: A micropredator.

Remarks: This fish has a voracious appetite and is a perennial roamer; it puts to rest the theory that substrate-spawning cichlids are territorial and only mouthbrooders are roamers. The much larger males steal and collect shells (sometimes with females inside) and lord over their pile, protecting the females who come to spawn in the shells.

Lamprologus lemairii
BOULENGER 1899

Size: 10 inches (25 cm) TL.

Dietary Notes: A piscivore.

Remarks: This is another highly predatory cichlid that is only suitable for large aquariums that contain other aggressive species. They are best kept alone, but due to their rather drab coloration, they don't make very good show specimens.

Lamprologus ocellatus
(Steindachner 1909)

| 7.8 | 8.0 | + |

Size: 2 inches (5 cm) TL.

Dietary Notes: A micropredator.

Remarks: This small shelldweller is often confused with a close relative—*Neolamprologus brevis*. They can be distinguished from *N. brevis* by the concave outline of the snout, which appears slightly caved in. The colors are not unattractive, but are altogether drab. As with other shell dwellers, it is best to keep only one male with multiple females and provide plenty of shells for them to hide in and among.

Lepidiolamprologus cunningtoni
(BOULENGER 1906)

Size: 11.5 inches (29 cm) TL.

Dietary Notes: A piscivore.

Remarks: As a rule, *L. cunningtoni* prefers to swim close to the sandy bottom, though the others in this genus seem to prefer hovering above the substrate. They make good tankmates for large aquariums with other predatory cichlid species.

Lepidiolamprologus elongatus
(Boulenger 1898)

Size: 13 inches (32.5 cm) TL; sometimes larger.

Dietary Notes: A piscivore.

Remarks: *L. elongatus* is the most common of the seven congeners. The others have been exported only sporadically at best, although captive-bred young are sometimes available from specialists.

Lepidiolamprologus kendalli
(POLL & STEWART 1977)

Size: 8 inches (20 cm) TL.

Dietary Notes: A piscivore.

Remarks: This species is similar to *L. elongatus* and another, less common species, *L. profundicola* in its solitary, rock-dwelling habit. Out of all of the fishes in the group, this one is probably the most colorful and interesting to look at.

Lepidiolamprologus nkambae
(STAECK 1978)

Size: 6 inches (15 cm) TL.

Dietary Notes: A piscivore.

Remarks: *Lepidiolamprologus nkambae* is slightly smaller than other members of the genus. In nature, they can usually be found hiding deep within the crevices of rocks. Their aquariums should contain caves constructed of rocks or anything else that will provide suitable cover. This species is native to the southern end of Lake Tanganyika.

Neolamprologus brevis
(Boulenger 1899)

Size: 2 inches (5 cm) TL.

Dietary Notes: A planktonivore.

Remarks: These little shelldwellers are fascinating to observe in the home aquarium. For the best show, keep two or three males with a small harem of females in a 20-gallon long aquarium. Provide a shell for each fish and watch the males battle harmlessly over which one gets more of the shells. Because all of the attention and aggression is focused on their shells, these tiny cichlids can often be kept in community tanks with various non cichlids.

Neolamprologus brichardi
(POLL 1974)

Trade Name: Princess of Burundi.

Size: 5 inches (12 cm) TL.

Dietary Notes: A planktonivore.

Remarks: In the lake hundreds of pairs form breeding colonies, and all the fish join in defense against predators. A spawning pair will commandeer even a large aquarium and are best bred in their own tank, where you will soon have fry of all ages living together.

Neolamprologus buescheri
(STAECK 1983)

| 7.8 | 8.0 | + |

Size: 5 inches (12 cm) TL.

Dietary Notes: A planktonivore.

Remarks: A deepwater species, these fish are difficult to bring to the surface alive because of their need for a slow decompression period. They are unmistakable, with their horizontal stripes, crescentic caudal fin, and a shape reminiscent of *N. furcifer*.

Neolamprologus caudopunctatus
(Poll 1978)
Size: 4 inches (10 cm) TL.

Neolamprologus cylindricus
Staeck & Seegers 1986
Size: 6 inches (15 cm) TL.

Neolamprologus falcicula
(Brichard 1989)
Size: 5 inches (12 cm) TL.

Neolamprologus fasciatus
(Boulenger 1898)
Size: 5 inches (12 cm) TL.

Neolamprologus furcifer
(Boulenger 1898)
Size: 6 inches (15 cm) TL.

Neolamprologus gracilis
(Brichard 1989)
Size: 3 inches (8 cm) TL.

Please see remarks opposite
for additional information.

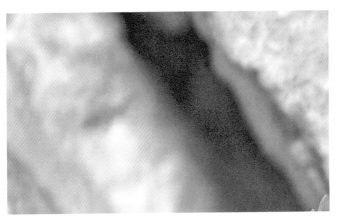

Neolamprologus helianthus
BÜSCHER 1997

 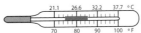

Trade Names: Sunflower brichardi.

Size: 4 inches (10 cm) TL.

Dietary Notes: A planktonivore.

Remarks: A relative newcomer to the trade, this attractively gold-spotted brichardi-type cichlid was an instant hit. It is now widely available.

Neolamprologus leloupi
(Poll 1948)
Size: 2.5 inches (6 cm) TL.

Neolamprologus mustax
(Poll 1978)
Size: 4 inches (10 cm) TL.

Neolamprologus niger
(Poll 1956)
Size: 4 inches (10 cm) TL.

Neolamprologus nigriventris
Büscher, 1992
Size: 4 inches (10 cm) TL.

Neolamprologus olivaceous
Büscher, 1992
Size: 4 inches (10 cm) TL.

Neolamprologus savoryi
(Poll 1949)
Size: 6 inches (15 cm) TL.

Please see remarks opposite
for additional information.

Neolamprologus leleupi
(POLL 1956)

Size: 6 inches (15 cm) TL.

Dietary Notes: A micropredator.

Remarks: This is one of the most popular cichlids from the lake. Various populations exist, ranging in color from yellowish brown to brilliant orange-yellow. A great fish to add a blast of bright yellow to a Tanganyikan community tank.

Neolamprologus pulcher
(TREWAVAS & POLL 1952)

Trade Names: Daffodil brichardi.

Size: 6 inches (15 cm) TL.

Dietary Notes: A planktonivore.

Remarks: This species was at first considered to be a subspecies of *N. savoryi*, but was set apart as a distinct species by Max Poll. It should not be maintained with other species of the brichardi complex to prevent hybridization.

Neolamprologus sexfasciatus
(TREWAVAS & POLL 1952)

Trade Name: Six-bar cichlid.

Size: 8 inches (20 cm) TL.

Dietary Notes: A micropredator.

Remarks: This is one of the most spectacular species of cichlid in Lake Tanganyika. It is distinguished from its close relatives by the fact that it has six dark bands, whereas *N. tretocephalus* has only five bands.

Neolamprologus tetracanthus
(BOULENGER 1899)

Size: 8 inches (20 cm) TL.

Dietary Notes: A generalized predator.

Remarks: This is one of the least specialized forms of *Neolamprologus*, found mainly on the sandy bottom all around the lake without any noticeable local races. Of all the sand-dwelling species in the lake, this species is one of the better-looking ones, and it is popular with hobbyists. They are prolific spawners, and it is not uncommon for hobbyists to raise many more fry than they will ever be able to give away or sell back to their local pet shop.

Neolamprologus toae
(POLL 1949)

Size: 6 inches (15 cm) TL.

Dietary Notes: Primarily an insectivore.

Remarks: In 1985 Colombe & Allgayer erected the monotypic genus *Paleolamprologus* for this fish, but this has not been widely accepted. It certainly is the case that this is an unusual lamp, even if it does not merit its own genus. Its most notable feature is the very large eye. Apparently it is a nocturnal predator. This species makes a fascinating addition to a collection of tangs.

Neolamprologus tretocephalus
(BOULENGER 1899)

Trade Name: Five-bar cichlid.

Size: 6 inches (15 cm) TL.

Dietary Notes: A molluscivore.

Remarks: These cichlids are very popular due to their unique bluish coloration. Adult males in good condition are sometimes purple along the edges of their fins. Their care and husbandry in aquariums are similar to other species in the genus.

Telmatochromis bifrenatus
MYERS 1936

Size: 3.5 inches (9 cm) TL.

Dietary Notes: Omnivorous.

Remarks: Feeds on aufwuchs and other cichlids' eggs. Looking similar to *Julidochromis* and *Chalinochromis*, these cichlids are small and peaceful. They live and spawn in tiny caves or in shells. A pair can be kept and bred in a very small tank, though you should watch out for intra-pair aggression.

Telmatochromis brichardi
Louisy 1989

Size: 2 inches (5 cm) TL.

Dietary Notes: Omnivorous.

Remarks: This small cichlid is fairly peaceful. Like many of its congeners, it specializes in eating other cichlids' eggs, though it also feeds off the aufwuchs. It is a shelldweller.

Telmatochromis dhonti
(BOULENGER 1919)

| 7.8 | 8.0 | + |

Size: 5 inches (12 cm) TL.

Dietary Notes: Mostly carnivorous; eats sponges.

Remarks: Unlike most of the fish in this genus, this is a highly aggressive cichlid. They are cave brooders by nature and will hide much of the time they are in your aquarium, only to dart out and attack unsuspecting passersby.

Cyphotilapines & Tropheines

The tropheines are maternal mouthbrooders, and most are herbivorous—algae, phytoplankton, and plant eaters. Those found in the rocky zones graze on algae-covered rocks. Traditionally considered tropheine, the genus *Cyphotilapia* is quite distinct from the others, and Takashi places them in their own tribe, Cyphotilapini. We follow that here without pursuing the taxonomic questions, since from the aquaristic point of view these two groups of fish are so different.

CYPHOTILAPINI

These spectacular fishes are denizens of the deep, living at depths just above the anoxic layer. They must be decompressed when brought to the surface, which led to their extremely high original prices. These are predators on small fishes, especially cyprichromine cichlids. Adapted to darker environs, they hunt early in the morning and at dusk, swallowing *Cyprichromis* that head for the lake bottom to sleep.

Natural History and Captive Husbandry

If you are used to other large piscivorous cichlids, you will find frontosas easy-going, even shy. They do not like bright light, movement outside their tank, or aggressive tankmates. They are also slow eaters (why would they need to hurry, with their prey asleep?), and usually cannot compete with boisterous tankmates for food.

Since they are large fish, they need equally large tanks. Keep the lighting subdued, and provide rocks, PVC sections, or large flowerpots for hiding spaces. They are generally quite peaceful toward other fish too large to eat, but males will battle; it is best to keep a single male with several females. These are schooling fish, and they are best kept in groups of at least four to six.

The male will excavate or claim a cave, into which he entices a female for spawning. Females hold the eggs and fry for a long time, during which they will feed, providing nourishment for themselves as well as for their brood.

Frontosa are large-growing cichlids that prefer dim lighting.

Cyphotilapia frontosa
(Boulenger 1906)
Size: 12 inches (30 cm).

Cyphotilapia gibberosa
Takahashi & Nakaya 2003
Size: 12 inches (30 cm).

***Cyphotilapia* sp. "Burundi"**
Size: 16 inches (40 cm).

***Cyphotilapia* sp. "Burundi"**
Size: 16 inches (40 cm).

***Cyphotilapia* sp. "Zaire Blue"**
Size: 12 inches (30 cm), may
grow slightly larger.

***Cyphotilapia* sp. "Zaire Blue"**
Size: 12 inches (30 cm), may
grow slightly larger.

Please see remarks on pages 158-159
regarding care and husbandry.

TROPHEINI

Once again we find a group of fishes that show enormous variation in pattern and coloration from population to population, especially in *Tropheus*. There is revision going on, of course, but it is clear that even with a strict definition of species, these are highly variable fish. There is no consensus about the potential for hybridization between different *Tropheus*. Some breeders claim that even two color varieties of the same species can be maintained in the same tank without interbreeding. It is always safest, however, when breeding any cichlids, to keep only one species/population/variety in a tank.

Natural History and Captive Husbandry

For the most part, these fish are herbivorous, either algae grazers or omnivores with a heavy vegetarian bent. These are the particular focus of arguments against feeding herbivorous cichlids a meat-based diet. These are also extremely aggressive animals, not so much toward other species, but toward their own and similar species. It is virtually impossible to keep a small number of them in an aquarium. Although some people succeed with 10, you will have a better chance of success starting with 20 or so—a high female-to-male ratio is important, too.

Some rockwork should be provided for hiding spaces, but most of the time these gregarious and boisterous fish will be swimming nonstop around the tank, looking for something to eat. Females holding eggs are more retiring, and due to the small brood size and high value of the fry.

Water quality is of utmost importance, and heavy-duty filtration and frequent water changes are vital. Although many try smaller tanks, a 75-gallon (283.5 l), 4-foot tank is about minimum for any of these fishes.

Lobochilotes labiatus
(BOULENGER 1898)

Size: 14.5 inches (37 cm).

Dietary Notes: Heavily herbivorous.

Remarks: With *Cyphotilapia* removed, this is the odd member of the tribe Tropheini. It is over a foot long, not very *Tropheus*-shaped, and it feeds on invertebrates, particularly mollusks. The large lips for which it is named suggest that it sucks a lot of its prey out of crevices among the rocks. It is very aggressive to all other fishes, conspecifics or not, and very large, so to keep a group of them would probably require a 10-foot aquarium. It is rarely available.

Petrochromis famula
MATTHES & TREWAVAS, 1960

Size: 6 inches (15 cm).

Dietary Notes: Algae grazer.

Remarks: This genus is extremely similar to *Tropheus*—in size, shape, diet, habit, aggressiveness, and captive care. It is also a genus of extremely variable populations for which the taxonomy is still not worked out. Many of the trade names are simply a location or color—or both, like *Petrochromis* sp. Moshi "Golden Mpimbwe."

163

Petrochromis polydon
BOULENGER 1898

Size: 10 inches (25 cm).
Dietary Notes: Algae grazer.
Remarks: This species is only available in small numbers. It is
noted for being fiercely aggressive, even compared to its
congeners.

Petrochromis trewavasae
POLL 1948

Size: 7 inches (18 cm).

Dietary Notes: Algae grazer.

Remarks: This species is becoming more popular, perhaps due to its reputation for being a bit less aggressive, meaning a group can actually be maintained in a very large tank with lots of rockwork.

Simochromis babaulti
PELLEGRIN 1927

| 7.8 | 8.0 | + |

Size: 4.25 inches (11 cm).

Dietary Notes: Algae grazer.

Remarks: The smallest member of the genus, this is a hardy, solitary species that is quite intolerant of conspecifics and of any other algae grazer.

Tropheus annectens
BOULENGER 1900

| 7.8 | 8.0 | + |

Size: 6 inches (15 cm).

Dietary Notes: Algae grazer.

Remarks: This genus is known for vastly different morphs at its different locations. *T. annectens* shows only a few variants and is perhaps the least common in the hobby. There is controversy over possible synonymy of this species with *T. polli*.

Tropheus brichardi
NELISSEN & THYS VAN DEN AUDENAERDE 1975

Size: 6 inches (15 cm).
Dietary Notes: Algae grazer.
Remarks: A highly variable and popular species, specimens can often be easily identified by their blue eyes.

Tropheus duboisi
MARLIER 1959

| 7.8 | 8.0 | + |

21.1 26.6 32.2 37.7 °C
70 80 90 100 °F

Trade Name: Duboisi.

Size: 6 inches (15 cm).

Dietary Notes: Algae grazer.

Remarks: There are two main types of *T. duboisi*, a broad yellow band variety and the "Maswa" variety. One of the first in this genus to become popular, the striking juveniles are black with white polka dots.

Tropheus moorii
BOULENGER 1898

Size: 4 inches (10 cm).
Dietary Notes: Algae grazer.
Remarks: This species has an enormous number of variant populations, all different, some exquisitely colored. Some of the morphs assigned to this species may wind up being described as distinct species, but it is certain there will still be plenty of variety in this one.

Tropheus polli
AXELROD 1977

Trade Name: Swallowtail Tropheus.

Size: 6 inches (15 cm).

Dietary Notes: Algae grazer.

Remarks: There is controversy over the validity of this species as compared with *T. annectens*, though there are strong arguments in favor of the two species. This lyre-tailed fish shows a bit more sexual dimorphism than most *Tropheus*.

Tropheus sp. "flame"
Size: 6 inches (15 cm).

Tropheus sp. "bemba"
Size: 6 inches (15 cm).

Tropheus sp. "kaiser"
Size: 6 inches (15 cm).

Tropheus sp. "sunspot"
Size: 6 inches (15 cm).

Tropheus sp. "cherryspot"
Size: 6 inches (15 cm).

Tropheus sp. "red"
Size: 6 inches (15 cm).

Please see remarks on page 161
regarding care and husbandry.

TROPHEUS VARIATION

A common trait among the Tropheini is considerable regional variation. In fact, identifying populations to the species level is not easy, and there is a great deal of controversy among taxonomists. Whatever the ultimate decisions, it is certain that even after the dust settles the genus *Tropheus* will contain species that have markedly different variants by locale.

Still, there is a gradation, with *T. duboisi* showing little variation (only two forms), *T. annectens* and *T. polli* having a few variants, and *T. brichardi* and *T. moorii* brimming with geographical variants. It remains to be seen if the undescribed forms wind up being identified as multiple variants of one or two species like *brichardi* and *moorii* or being placed in several relatively invariant species like *duboisi* and *annectens*. The genus has more than 120 discovered variants, so no matter the final number of species, there will be a lot of regional morphs.

While the base color of *Tropheus* is generally dark brown or gray, variants exist with just about any other colors superimposed on the drab background. Although in the case of *duboisi* the two variants differ basically in the width of the medial band, *brichardi* and *moorii* variants have coloring book variants—they look as if blank outlines of the fish were distributed to a large elementary class, who went to town with their jumbo box of crayons.

Some morphs known as "rainbows" have subtle gradients of colors, while others sport stark contrasts like red bellies, two round red dots, yellow blotches, colored dorsal fins, etc. Many morphs demonstrate a marked difference in coloration between the fry and the adults. The most famous example is the polka dot juvenile coloration of *duboisi*, but there are many other instances, including a morph with bright red fry.

Biologists are working to determine the origin of all these variants. There appear to be too many to be accounted for with the biogeohistory of the lake, and while the different morphs do exhibit some reproductive isolation when brought together, there are still many unanswered questions. Hobbyist's experience with hybridization among *Tropheus* is quite varied, but there is an easy solution: ignore the disagreement. In other words, there are powerful arguments for preserving natural breeding populations as much as is possible in captivity. That means that whether any particular morphs are different species or different color morphs of one species, they should not be housed together.

Non-Rock Dwelling Tanganikans

This chapter covers an admittedly *ad hoc* grouping of cichlids—the leftovers. Nevertheless, they are all usually associated with sandy areas; some of them live on the sand, and some are fish that swim in open water over sandy areas. The habits and habitats of these cichlids differ widely, so we will cover their natural history and captive husbandry on a tribal basis.

Ectodini

These cichlids can be treated as two groups, the featherfins and the sandsifting cichlids, though some species are intermediate. The name "featherfin" is applied fairly regularly to *Ophthalmotilapia* and *Cyathopharynx*, and occasionally to other genera as well.

Natural History & Captive Husbandry

The featherfins are generally planktonivores and are typically found in schools above sandy areas. These species are noted for the spectacular sandpit nests the males build. The featherfins are open-water cichlids, spending much of their time foraging over sandy bottoms. Some feed primarily on drifting plankton, while others also pick at small invertebrates and probably some algae, too.

Many of the other species in this tribe are much more closely tied to the sandy bottom. These have a more goby-like body shape and often perch on the sand directly. Their typical manner of obtaining food is to sift sand for invertebrates and other edibles. These species do not build such extravagant nests, but they defend breeding territories and are generally maternal mouthbrooders like the featherfins.

Observing the breeding behaviors of featherfins would be sufficient motivation to keep them even if they didn't have beautiful coloration. The males build their sand bowers, and in some cases, a fish will take all of the sand in his tank, no matter how much is added, and build a spawning platform almost to the water surface! Some species form leks, with their crater nests gathered in one area, equally spaced from each other. When breeding, the males develop swollen knobs at the ends of their long pelvic fins. They drag these across the bottom of their nests as part of their courtship display; it is believed the females perceive them as eggs and come in to pick them up. In addition, after spawning, the females peck on these knobs, signaling the male to emit milt, increasing the likelihood of fertilizing the eggs in her mouth. In fact, in some cases females have been observed to lay eggs and pick them up, and only then seek out a male and tug on the fins to fertilize the eggs.

Many of Lake Tanganyika's featherfins exhibit striking coloration.

175

Aulonocranus dewindti
(BOULENGER 1899)

Size: 5.5 inches (14 cm) TL.
Dietary Notes: A semi-pelagic planktonivore.
Remarks: A monotypic genus. This featherfin is found in
schools of hundreds of fish over sandy bottoms. Also found
in Rusisi and Luguka Rivers. The male builds a crater nest.

Callochromis macrops
(BOULENGER 1898)

Size: 5.5 inches (14 cm) TL.

Dietary Notes: A sand sifter.

Remarks: Usually found in schools. The big eye and flat belly of this species is typical for the genus. Males develop beautiful iridescent colors on their sides.

Callochromis melanostigma
(BOULENGER 1906)

Size: 6 inches (15 cm) TL.

Dietary Notes: A micropredator.

Remarks: Black spots in the dorsal fin distinguish this species. The big eye and flat belly of this species is typical for the genus. Males develop beautiful iridescent colors on their sides.

Cyanthopharynx furcifer
(Boulenger 1898)

Size: 9 inches (23 cm) TL.

Dietary Notes: A planktonivore.

Remarks: Although you will read about distinguishing two species, *C. foae* and *C. furcifer*, each with several color morphs, there are intermediate forms as well. It is not certain that the genus will remain monotypic. The care of all these featherfins is the same.

Ophthalmotilapia boops
(BOULENGER 1910)

Size: 5.5 inches (14 cm) TL.

Dietary Notes: A planktonivore.

Remarks: The featherfins of this genus are quite popular and easily found in the hobby. The males' sand bower nests are quite spectacular.

Xenotilapia flavipinnis
POLL 1985

Size: 4 inches (10 cm) TL.

Dietary Notes: A micropredator.

Remarks: This small Tanganyikan cichlid does best on a sandy substrate in small groups. They are a biparental mouthbrooding where the female broods the eggs and fry for approximately 9 days after which the male takes over for the remaining time, which is usually about 5 to 6 days. A delicate and fairly peaceful cichlid, this and its congeners are often considered inchesgoby cichlids inches along with the Eretmodini. Several species/morphs are popular in the hobby.

CYPRICHROMINI

These cichlids have adapted completely to life in the water column, to the extent that they do not even use a substrate for spawning. Males defend a three-dimensional territory with invisible boundaries—they space themselves out above, below, and next to one another and court females as they swim by.

Spawning takes place in midwater, the male fertilizing eggs as they are laid, and the female picking them up before they fall away from the pair.

Natural History & Captive Husbandry

These cichlids live in large schools, feeding on plankton and spending their entire lives up in the water column. At night they sink toward the bottom, where they are preyed upon by *Cyphotilapia*. They should be kept only in groups, preferably in a large group in a large tank. They are delicate and very peaceful, and they do not ship well.

They will take prepared foods, but they should be fed often. Best is to supply baby brine shrimp or small daphnia so they can feed naturally over a prolonged period.

Cyprichromis are important food fishes for large piscivores, such as *Cyphotilapia*.

Cyprichromis leptosoma
(Boulenger 1898)
Size: 4.25 inches (11 cm) TL.

Cyprichromis leptosoma
(Boulenger 1898)
Size: 4.25 inches (11 cm) TL.

Cyprichromis leptosoma
(Boulenger 1898)
Size: 4.25 inches (11 cm) TL.

Cyprichromis leptosoma
(Boulenger 1898)
Size: 4.25 inches (11 cm) TL.

Cyprichromis leptosoma
(Boulenger 1898)
Size: 4.25 inches (11 cm) TL.

Paracyprichromis nigripinnis
(Boulenger 1901)
Size: 4.25 inches (11 cm) TL.

Please see remarks on page opposite
regarding care and husbandry.

ERETMODINI

These cichlids, called inchesgoby cichlids inches are even more adapted to benthic life than are the Ectodini sand sifters. They are small and fairly plain, though neon blue polka dots and various dark markings break up their silver coloration. The taxonomy of the group has been called into question by DNA studies, and it is likely that some changes will be made.

Natural History & Captive Husbandry

This tribe has made full adaptation to the sandy and pebbly bottoms of the surge zone—where waves crash against the shore. The water here is 3 feet or less in depth, turbulent, and extremely well oxygenated. Their non functional swim bladders make them less buoyant, and their body is shaped to hug the bottom. They have underslung mouths for grazing the abundant algae and aufwuchs that grow on the rocks in this shallow water. Their dorsal fins are very spiny—a deterrent to fishing birds.

These small cichlids make excellent aquarium specimens, and what they lack in coloration they make up for in comical personality. They do not, however, ship well because of their high oxygen demands. To keep them successfully, maximum oxygen saturation must be maintained at all times. Powerheads, canister filters, and protein skimmers can be used effectively to maximize gas exchange in a goby cichlid aquarium. Airstones are a poor second choice.

These fish can be territorially aggressive, and despite their small size, a large aquarium is best, with plenty of hiding spots. In contrast to the goby-like Ectodini, the Eretmodini do not school and are found singly or in pairs. They are biparental mouthbrooders, with the male typically taking up the last 10 days of the 20-day incubation.

Eretmodus cyanosticus
Boulenger 1898
Size: 3.5 inches (9 cm) TL.

Eretmodus cyanosticus
Boulenger 1898
Size: 3.5 inches (9 cm) TL.

Spathodus marlieri
Poll 1950
Size: 4 inches (10 cm) TL.

Spathodus marlieri
Poll 1950
Size: 4 inches (10 cm) TL.

Spathodus erythrodon
Boulenger 1900
Size: 3.5 inches (8.5 cm) TL.

Tanganicodus irsacae
Poll 1950
Size: 2.75 inches (7 cm) TL.

Please see remarks on page opposite
regarding care and husbandry.

185

LIMNOCHROMINI

This tribe contains medium-sized deepwater species that are biparental or maternal mouthbrooders. Some are quite attractively colored. Some species are highly aggressive. Many show affinity to cyprochromines, both in form and habit.

Takashi places *Greenwoodochromis* into its own tribe Greenwoodochromini, and *Benthochromis* into its own, Benthochromini.

Natural History & Captive Husbandry

These fishes are from deep water, and wild-caught animals need careful decompression. Once acclimated, however, they adapt well to the aquarium. They are opportunistically omnivorous, grabbing plankton, algae, crustaceans, and insects as they patrol the deeps.

Benthochromis tricoti
(Poll 1948)
Size: 6.75 inches (17 cm) TL.

Greenwoodochromis christyi
(Trewavas 1953)
Size: 6 inches (15 cm) TL.

Limnochromis auritus
(Boulenger 1901)
Size: 5 inches (13 cm) TL.

Reganochromis calliurus
(Boulenger 1901)
Size: 6 inches (15 cm) TL.

Benthochromis tricoti is by far the most commonly kept species of the tribe Limnochromini.

TYLOCHROMINI

The single genus in this tribe contains approximately 19 species. However, only one (*T. polylepis*) is found in the lake. They are all large, rather drab, and rarely imported.

Natural History & Captive Husbandry

Since these fish are very large and can be very aggressive, an aquarium of several hundred gallons minimum would be necessary to maintain a group. Since they are maternal mouthbrooders, several females and a male would be the recommended way to proceed.

HAPLOCHROMINI

Recent genetic studies (Salzburger, Mack, Verheyen, and Meyer) have demonstrated that Lake Tanganyika was the origin of the haplochromines, which spread from the lake into the rivers. The Tropheini are, in turn, derived from riverine haplochromines and are secondary colonizers of the lake. While all of the endemic cichlids of Malawi and Victoria are haps, the tribe Haplochromini is virtually absent in Tanganyika. A handful of species occur in the lake, associated with various rivers and their swamps, but the haplochromine tribe is a more modern lineage associated mainly with rivers and the younger lakes. You might say that the haps that stayed in Lake Tanganyika all evolved into something else.

Natural History & Captive Husbandry

These cichlids show great affinity to other haplochromines, such as Victorian cichlids. They are moderately aggressive maternal mouthbrooders, meaning they should be maintained for breeding in large single-species tanks with groups of several females to every male.

Astatoreochromis straeleni
(POLL 1944)

Size: 4.75 inches (12 cm) TL.
Dietary Notes: An omnivore.
Remarks: This cichlid and its congener *A. vanderhorsti* (GREENWOOD 1954) are found in the lake only in the swamps and at the mouths of rivers.

Astatotilapia burtoni
(GÜNTHER 1894)

| 7.8 | 8.0 | + |

Size: 6 inches (15 cm) TL.
Dietary Notes: An omnivore.
Remarks: Another riverine species that is found in the lake near rivers. This cichlid is also found in Lake Kivu.

PERISSODINI

These cichlids practice lepidophagy—eating scales. They typically sneak up from behind, lunge, and swim off with a mouthful of scales. The fish digests the skin and flesh attached the scales, as well as the mucus slime. The bony scale itself passes through undigested.

Their specific adaptations include specially shaped mouths and even "handedness," in which the mouth is skewed to one side to facilitate feeding from the opposite side; that is, a fish with a mouth skewed to the left will attack the right side of fish.

For all this preparedness, their lives are not easy. Other cichlids learn quickly to watch out for these nasty characters, and the scale eaters are successful in getting a meal in only one in five attempts.

Natural History & Captive Husbandry

Obviously it is risky to maintain these fish in a community tank, but aquarists report that they do not attack tankmates they have been raised with. They are biparental mouthbrooders and have rather large spawns. They will feed well on any carnivorous diet and do not need scales in their diet. Some of the species are quite large and require spacious accommodations.

Plecodus species are accomplished scale-eaters and should not be kept in community aquariums.

Plecodus straeleni
POLL 1948

Size: 6.25 inches (16 cm) TL.

Dietary Notes: Feeds by ripping scales off other fish.

Remarks: A solitary cichlid that is not recommended for community aquariums due to their scale-eating habits.

BATHYBATINI

Takashi includes *Trematocara* in this tribe, while in Poll's analysis there are two genera in Bathybatini and one in the separate tribe Trematocarini. These are all deepwater species that are maternal mouthbrooders. They are predators, usually feeding on small fishes. The first two genera listed here are large fish, with the smallest species being a foot in length. The *Trematocara* are comparative dwarfs, ranging from 3 to 6 inches depending on species.

Natural History & Captive Husbandry

These deepwater species adapt well to aquarium life once acclimated. Since most species are large, schooling fishes, large tanks are necessary. Their predatory habits make them poor choices for community tanks.

Bathybates are voracious piscivores in their natural habitat. *B. fasciatus is* pictured here.

Bathybates fasciatus
BOULENGER 1901

Size: 16 inches (40 cm) TL.
Dietary Notes: A piscivorous predator.
Remarks: Hunts in schools for small fishes, especially clupeids.

Bathybates vittatus
BOULENGER 1914

Size: 16.5 inches (42 cm) TL.

Dietary Notes: A piscivorous predator.

Remarks: Hunts in schools for small fishes, especially clupeids.

Chapter 6

Region 4
Lake Victoria
Basin

Lake Victoria is the second largest lake in the world in surface area, but it is relatively shallow—a maximum depth of only about 270 feet (82 meters) compared to 2300 feet for Malawi and 4800 feet for Tanganyika.

Known as both Darwin's Dream Pond and Darwin's Nightmare, Lake Victoria is a true marvel of nature, and its endemic cichlids are—or in many cases *were*—fascinating as well. In a mere blink of a geologic eye, cichlids speciated into an enormous flock, but in a mere few years, at the hand of our species, this biological treasure has been ransacked.

To comprehend what was lost, one must first know what once was. Technically, Victoria is not a rift lake; it formed in the hollow created by the uplifting of the East and West Rifts in Africa. As mentioned, it is very shallow, with a maximum depth of 270 feet (82 meters) and an average depth of only half that. It drains into Lake Edward, and together they are the source of the Nile River.

The ichthyofauna is not the same in Lake Victoria as in her satellite lakes Albert, Edward, Kyogo, and Kivu, but there is overlap. Often fish from any of these habitats are treated in the hobby as "Victorians." Victoria is much larger than any of the others; still, some of the cichlids in the trade are from the smaller lakes.

HAPLOCHROMINI

When the color of a Victorian cichlid is described, it is understood that we are talking about a male in breeding dress. Immature males, females, and subdominant males that are trying to avoid the tank's dominant male's attention are drab silver fish in almost all cases.

Astatoreochromis alluaudi
Pellegrin 1904
Size: 7.5 inches (19 cm) TL.

Astatotilapia aeneocolor
(Greenwood 1973)
Size: 5 inches (13 cm) TL.

Astatotilapia nubila
(Boulenger 1906)
Size: 3.5 inches (9 cm) TL.

Enterochromis sp.
Size: 3.5 inches (9 cm) TL.

Please see remarks opposite
regarding care and husbandry.

Natural History & Captive Husbandry

The lake has a definite thermocline and turns over completely every year. The water temperature varies between 70°F (21°C) and 81°F (27°C). The pH is typically between 7.2 and 8.6 and conductivity 100 to 150 µS. The use of buffer salts and/or soluble rocks and substrate will help maintain conditions favorable to these species.

Almost all haps are opportunistic feeders, though a few species have extremely specialized diets. Nevertheless, most all will do well on a general omnivorous diet. A cichlid pellet based on spirulina is excellent. Remember that even the carnivorous species eat things in the wild that have themselves eaten algae, and the bright colors of the male are often based on substances derived from plant sources, so feeding veggies will often brighten the colors of the fish.

It's very important to offer all captive Victorian fishes plant material in their diet, as they are generally omnivorous feeders in nature.

Haplochromis ishmaeli
Boulenger 1906
Size: 5.5 inches (14 cm) TL.

***Haplochromis* sp. "all red"**
Trade Names: Kyoga flameback.
Size: 6 inches (15 cm) TL.

***Haplochromis* sp. "fine bar scraper"**
Size: 4.5 inches (11.5 cm) TL.

***Haplochromis* sp. "flameback"**
Size: 5 inches (13 cm) TL.

***Haplochromis* sp. "Hippo Point salmon"**
Size: 5.5 inches (14 cm) TL.

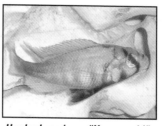

***Haplochromis* sp. "Kenya gold"**
Size: 3 inches (8 cm) TL

Please see remarks opposite
for additional information.

Astatotilapia latifasciata
(REGAN 1929)

| 7.6 | 7.8 | 8.0 |

Trade Names: *Haplochromis obliquidens*, *H.* "zebra obliquidens."
Size: 4.25" (11 cm) TL.
Dietary Notes: An insectivore.
Remarks: This haplochromine is found in Lakes Kyoga and Nawampasa north of Victoria in Uganda. Long known as *Haplochromis obliquidens*, this is not that species. The females are unusual in being colored similarly to the males, who have the same barred pattern but also with a red belly.

Haplochromis sp. "red tail sheller"
Size: 5.5 inches (14 cm) TL.

Haplochromis sp. "ruby green"
Size: 3.75 inches (9.5 cm) TL.

Haplochromis sp. "thick skin"
Size: 5 inches (13 cm) TL.

Haplochromis sp. "Uganda red"
Size: 4.5 inches (11.5 cm) TL.

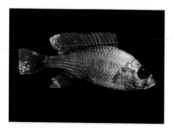

Haplochromis sp.
Size: 5 inches (13 cm) TL.

Paralabidochromis chromogynos
(Greenwood 1959)
Size: 4.5 inches (11 cm) TL.

Please see remarks on page 201
for additional information.

Lipochromis parvidens
(Boulenger 1911)
Size: 6 inches (15 cm) TL.

Lithochromis rufus
Seehausen & Lippitsch 1998
Size: 3.5 inches (9 cm) TL.

Mbipia lutea
Seehausen & Bouton 1998
Size: 5 inches (13 cm) TL.

Neochromis nigricans
(Boulenger 1906)
Size: 5 inches (12.5 cm) TL.

Paralabidochromis chilotes
(Boulenger 1911)
Size: 6 inches (15 cm) TL.

***Haplochromis* sp. "piebald"**
(Greenwood 1959)
Size: 4.5 inches (11 cm) TL.

Please see remarks on page 201
for additional information.

203

***Paralabidochromis* sp. "rock kribensis"**
Size: 5 inches (13 cm) TL.

***Pundamilia* sp. "blue bar"**
Size: 3 inches (8 cm) TL.

Pundamilia nyererei
(Witte-Maas & Witte 1985)
Size: 3 inches (8 cm) TL.

Pyxichromis orthostoma
(Regan 1922)
Size: 8 inches (20 cm) TL.

Xystichromis phytophagus
Greenwood 1966
Size: 4 inches (10 cm) TL.

***Haplochromis* sp.**
Undescribed to date
Size: 5 inches (13 cm) TL.

Please see remarks on page 201 for additional information.

TILAPIINI

A couple of tilapiine cichlids are native to Lake Victoria. Although they are vastly outnumbered by haplochromine cichlid species (about 500 to 2), you may find *Oreochromis esculentus* on occasion.

Oreochromis esculentus
(GRAHAM 1928)

Trade Names: Ngege (native name).

Size: 20" (50 cm) TL.

Dietary Notes: A detritivore.

Remarks: Believed to be extinct in Victoria, this substrate spawner is a pest in areas in which it has been introduced. It is not commonly kept in aquaria, but it needs very large ones when it is.

Chapter 7

Region 5
West Africa

The Crater
Lakes

The crater lakes of West Africa, principally in Cameroon, are the source for a number of cichlids, many of them endemic to their particular lake. Certainly important to the hobby, these fish are also extremely important to science, since they are examples of sympatric speciation. In almost all cases, the radiation of the cichlids in the African Great Lakes involved geographic separation, even if only because the fish will not cross open water, so that even nearby rocky reefs represent habitats isolated from each other.

These habitats are extremely precarious. When species are endemic to single tiny lakes, they can be exterminated by a single disaster, natural or manmade. Some of these crater lakes face immediate threat from pollution and habitat degradation, but even the more remote lakes are vulnerable. In addition to endemic species of non endemic genera, there are four genera of cichlids found only in the crater lakes: *Koina*, *Myaka*, *Pungu*, and *Stomatepia*.

It does not take a volcanic eruption to kill off the fish in a crater lake—a burp could do it. In 1986, Lake Nyos in Cameroon turned, something it does not normally do. The carbon dioxide dissolved in the deepest layers effervesced to the surface and spread out more than 10 miles around the mountain, asphyxiating 1700 people and their livestock.

Natural History & Captive Husbandry

The lakes tend to be of unusual chemical makeup, namely soft and basic. Fortunately, the cichlids from these habitats are quite adaptable to different water chemistries. Many of them make great aquarium specimens and breed readily in captivity.

Even the substrate spawners typically have small broods. The confines of the habitat require limited fecundity, but this also contributes to their rareness in the hobby. A couple dozen fry at a time is a hard way to build up a population. Their precariousness in the wild should motivate us to do everything we can to establish breeding populations in captivity. Little is known about most of these species, so this is a real opportunity for some pioneering.

Tilapia discolor **is another intresting cichlid species that is similar to other members of the genus.**

LAKE BAROMBI-MBO

A mere 1.7 square miles (4.5 km^2), this crater lake is home to 11 endemic cichlid species. Four of the five cichlid genera are endemic. These are *Sarothedon*-based maternal mouthbrooders. This habitat is currently threatened by overfishing, alien species introductions, deforestation and silting, and pollution from the rapidly growing city of Kumba. All of its cichlids are critically endangered.

Konia eisentrauti
(TREWAVAS 1962)

6.8	7.0	7.2

Size: 4 inches (10 cm) TL.

Dietary Notes: Omnivorous micropredator.

Remarks: This shallow water species is a bit more easily found in the hobby than its congener, but still not widespread. It is a mouthbrooder, and either male or female may take up the eggs.

Myaka myaka
Trewavas 1972

| 6.8 | 7.0 | 7.2 |

Size: 4 inches (10 cm) TL.

Dietary Notes: A planktonivore.

Remarks: Another monotypic, endemic genus, this fish is strikingly dichromatic in its breeding dress, with coppery black males and silvery white females. It is rather aggressive.

Pungu maclerini
(TREWAVAS 1962)

Size: 4.75 inches (12 cm) TL.

Dietary Notes: Diet includes sponges and terrestrial plants.

Remarks: A monotypic, endemic genus. This critically endangered fish is in the hobby, but not in any numbers. It is reported to be a maternal mouthbrooder.

Sarotherodon linnellii
(LÖNNBERG 1903)

Size: 10 inches (25 cm) TL.

Dietary Notes: Feeds on invertebrates and phytoplankton.

Remarks: Mature animals can show considerable metallic green coloration. They prefer food that is tiny, like baby brine shrimp. It is a maternal mouthbrooder.

Sarotherodon lohbergeri
(HOLLY 1930)

6.8	7.0	7.2

Size: 6 inches (15 cm) TL.

Dietary Notes: An algae and aufwuchs grazer.

Remarks: A schooling fish. Reported to be a biparental mouthbrooder with strong pair bonds.

Stomatepia pindu
TREWAVAS 1972

6.8	7.0	7.2

Size: 3.5 inches (9 cm) TL.
Dietary Notes: A predator. Diet includes shrimps.
Remarks: This hard-to-find species is one of the rare all-black cichlids.

Lake Bermin

This tiny crater lake (0.2 square miles, 0.5 km^2—this is the area of a circle just under 675 feet in diameter) has a flock of 9 tilapiine cichlids! The lake even has an endemic piscivorous colubrid snake—*Afronatrix anoscopus*. Fortunately, the fish are small and not utilized by the local people, and the lake is still quite isolated, but deforestation is an imminent threat. Many have bright red and yellow coloration, at least when breeding. A bright white lower lip is a common feature. All of the species in this micro flock are biparental substrate spawners.

Tilapia bythobates
STIASSNY, SCHLIEWEN & DOMINEY 1992

6.8	7.0	7.2

Size: 6 inches (15 cm) TL.

Dietary Notes: Herbivorous.

Remarks: American aquarists have had mixed success with this beautiful species. Hopefully it will soon become more widely available.

LAKE BOSUMTWI

This fascinating lake is the only natural lake in the country of Ghana. It is believed to have been formed by a meteorite strike between 1 and 2 million years ago. It has a surface area of 19 square miles (49 km2) and has no outlet—it is classified as a soda lake and has a conductivity of almost 1000 ìS (640 ppm). The lake is threatened by, among other things, the prospect of a Canadian company mining for gold in the area.

Hemichromis frempongi
LOISELLE 1979

6.8	7.0	7.2

Size: 10 inches (25 cm) TL. **Dietary Notes:** A predator.

Remarks: This endemic cichlid appears intermediate between a five-spot *Hemichromis* like *H. elongatus* and a red jewel species like *H. lifalili*, with the red on the belly covering a greater area of the basic five-spot coloration.

LAKE EJAGHAM

This crater lake in northwest Cameroon is not even on most lists of African lakes, so there cannot be much known about it. It has about half a dozen cichlid species as well as a couple of killifish and a barb. An endemic tilapia is present in the hobby:

Tilapia deckerti
THYS VAN DEN AUDENAERDE 1967

Size: 8 inches (20 cm) TL.

Dietary Notes: Probably omnivorous.

Remarks: An extremely variable fish, its breeding coloration is a beautiful iridescent black. It often displays brilliant blue lips. It is thought there is actually a sympatric species pair here, or perhaps evidence of speciation in action.

LAKE NATRON

This lake is not a crater lake; it is a soda (alkaline) lake on the floor of the Rift Valley in Kenya. We include it here just as an example of the diversity and adaptability of our favorite fish family Cichlidae. The only species of cichlid endemic to this lake is the alkaline tilapia, *Oreochromis* (*Tilapia, Alcolapia*) *alcalicus*.

Oreochromis alcalicus
(HILGENDORF 1905)

6.8	7.0	7.2

Size: 4.75 inches (12 cm) TL.

Dietary Notes: Feeds on blue-green algae and copepods.

Remarks: Extremely high sodium carbonate concentrations and temperatures of 86° to 90°F (30° to 32°C) make Lake Natron inhospitable to higher plants and most fishes, but cyanobacteria, a few invertebrates, and this cichlid thrive there. It is likely this species will be split, as there appears to be a very small species flock here.

Tilapia buttikoferi is one of the most popular West African cichlids. Read about it on page 257.

Riverine Cichlids

The vagaries of fate are evident in the waxing and waning popularity of West African cichlids in the hobby over the years. In the early days, the only cichlids from Africa were a few West African riverine species. Then, the Rift Lake explosion took place, and soon the term "African cichlid" came to mean a fish from one of the Great Lakes—Malawi, Tanganyika, or Victoria. Long-time favorites like the krib *Pelvicachromis pulcher* were all but forgotten.

The rivers of West Africa vary greatly in water chemistry. There are clearwater, blackwater, and whitewater streams and rivers. Conductivity varies from negligible (3 ìS) to quite hard (500 ìS), with a pH ranging from 4 to 9.5, depending on both location and time of year. Many cichlids have a wide distribution and are quite adaptable. On the other hand, others are found only in specific habitats, and these require more attention to water chemistry, at least for successful spawning. These will be noted in the listings below.

CHROMIDOTILAPIINI

Mitochondrial DNA studies support the monophyly of this tribe, which contains several genera and many species, including some beloved old-timers. Many chromidotilapiines are quite colorful. There are no really large cichlids in this group, and it includes some properly dwarf species. All are potential aquarium specimens.

There is a great deal of variation in this group, found in various habitats and breeding as polygamous maternal and monogamous biparental mouthbrooders as well as paternal mouthbrooders and cave spawners. Courting is typically initiated by females, who develop a very swollen belly with prominent genital papillae and a bright red or violet belly blotch.

Natural History & Aquarium Husbandry

Most chromidotilapiines come from soft, neutral to acid waters, but many of them will thrive and reproduce successfully in a wide range of water chemistries, including hard and basic. They are generally opportunistically omnivorous and should have considerable vegetable matter in their diets. Some—for example many *Chromidotilapia* species—also sift sand for detritus.

Chromidotilapia females develop a very swollen belly with a bright red or violet belly blotch.

Benitochromis batesi
(BOULENGER 1901)

Size: 4.75 inches (12 cm) TL.
Dietary Notes: Omnivorous.
Remarks: This genus was erected by Lamboj in 2001 out of
Chromidotilapia and some newly discovered species. This
species is the only larvophilic mouthbrooder in the genus.
Eggs are protected in a cave, then (usually) the female picks
up the larvae. Both parents protect the fry for about a month
after release. This species requires soft, acid water for
successful breeding.

Benitochromis finleyi
(TREWAVAS 1974)

Size: 4.75 inches (12 cm) TL.
Dietary Notes: Omnivorous.
Remarks: Pleasantly colored in pastel rose and blue, this species typically practices biparental mouthbrooding, with exchanges of eggs between parents several times a day.

Chromidotilapia guntheri
(SAUVAGE 1882)

Size: 6 inches (15 cm) TL.

Dietary Notes: Omnivorous.

Remarks: This is an old favorite—one of the first African cichlids in the hobby. The genus is large and perhaps polyphyletic. This species is unusual in that the male alone broods the eggs while the female guards the territory. After release, they both protect the fry, and the female also may at this time allow the young into her mouth.

Divandu albimarginatus
LAMBOJ & SNOEKS 2000

| 6.8 | 7.0 | 7.2 |

Size: 3 inches (8 cm) TL.

Dietary Notes: Feeds mainly on detritus, also sifts sand.

Remarks: A monotypic genus. This yellowish-brown cichlid has most of its color in its fins—reds, blues, and purples. It is quite aggressive toward conspecifics and is reported to be a larvophilic maternal mouthbrooder.

Nanochromis dimidiatus
(PELLEGRIN 1900)

6.8	7.0	7.2

Size: 2.75 inches (7 cm) TL.

Dietary Notes: Omnivorous.

Remarks: Considerable confusion has existed about the identity of this species since its original popularity in the 1960s, and this may be a species complex. This genus needs soft, neutral to acid water for spawning. Males are typically larger, and the sexes usually differ in coloration. They are all cave spawners.

Nanochromis parilus
ROBERTS & STEWART 1976

Size: 3.5 inches (9 cm) TL.

Dietary Notes: Omnivorous.

Remarks: Probably the most common species of this genus in the hobby, it is the most adaptable to different water conditions and can be spawned successfully in hard, basic water.

227

Nanochromis transvestitus
ROBERTS & STEWART 1984

Size: 2.5 inches (6 cm) TL.

Dietary Notes: Omnivorous.

Remarks: This specific name refers to the brighter coloration of the females—unusual for cichlids, but not for chromidotilapiines. This species requires soft, acid water, even just for maintenance.

Parananochromis longirostris
(BOULENGER 1903)

Size: 6 inches (15 cm) TL.

Dietary Notes: Feeds primarily on algae and aufwuchs.

Remarks: This is the only species in the genus that can be bred in hard, basic water. Despite earlier reports of mouthbrooding, this fish is a cave spawner.

Pelvicachromis humilis
(Boulenger 1916)
Size: 5 inches (12 cm) TL.

Pelvicachromis roloffi
(Thys van den Audenaerde
1968)
Size: 3 inches (8 cm) TL.

Pelvicachromis rubrolabiatus
Lamboj 2004
Size: 4 inches (10 cm) TL.

Pelvicachromis cf. *suboccelatus*
Size: 4 inches (10 cm) TL.

Pelvicachromis taeniatus
(Boulenger 1901)
Size: 3 inches (8 cm) TL.

Pelvicachromis taeniatus
(Boulenger 1901)
Size: 3 inches (8 cm) TL.

Please see remarks opposite
for additional information.

Pelvicachromis pulcher
(BOULENGER 1901)

Trade Names: Kribensis, krib.

Size: 4 inches (10 cm) TL.

Dietary Notes: Feeds primarily on algae and detritus.

Remarks: Found in Benin, Nigeria, and Cameroon. This is the krib, a fish perennially popular for many decades. Various aquarium strains exist, including an albino morph.

Teleogramma brichardi
POLL 1959

6.8	7.0	7.2

Size: 4.75 inches (12 cm) TL.

Dietary Notes: Feeds primarily on small invertebrates.

Remarks: There are four described species in this genus, all similar and highly reophilic, from rapids in the Congo River. At first glance these fish seem out of place with other chromidotilapiines, with their elongate shape, reduced swim bladder, and—very rare among cichlids—single lateral line. The female's red belly and courtship of the male, however, are typical of the group. Give them plenty of caves and heavy water movement.

HAPLOCHROMINI

This tribe is definitely the star of East Africa, with probably close to 1000 species just between Lakes Malawi and Victoria. As we mentioned, it is believed to have originated anciently in Lake Tanganyika and radiated out from there. As you might expect with such a large group, they show a great deal of diversity in morphology and in behavior. They all have in common being maternal mouthbrooders. Most are sexually dimorphic, with larger, more colorful males. Egg spots on the anal (and sometimes other) fins are very common to this group.

This tribe has a handful of species that inhabit the lakes and rivers of Western Africa. Some of these species also occur in Eastern Africa. None of the western species are currently in the hobby.

Natural History & Aquarium Husbandry

Most of these cichlids are medium to large, and many have wide ranges and can tolerate various water conditions. Most are opportunistic feeders and will accept just about any foods and thrive on them. Aggressiveness varies, but most can be maintained in polygynous groups in large tanks.

Ctenochromis horei is not to be confused with *C. luluae*, as the former is endemic to Lake Tanganyika.

Ctenochromis luluae
(FOWLER 1931)

6.8	7.0	7.2

Size: 4 inches (10 cm) TL.

Dietary Notes: Omnivorous

Remarks: Two of the five described species in this genus occur in Lake Tanganyika. The three western riverine species are rather drab but pleasant little cichlids. The females take the fry back in their mouths for up to a week following the first release.

Thoracochromis brauschi
(POLL & THYS VAN DEN AUDENAERDE, 1965)

6.8	7.0	7.2

Size: 5.5 inches (14 cm) TL.

Dietary Notes: Feeds mostly on higher plants.

Remarks: One of 18 species in the genus, this fish from the Congo drainage is a particularly attractive one, in which the red throat coloring for which the genus is named is particularly noticeable. Here is another hardy and adaptable fish—a fine prospect for the aquarium hobby.

HEMICHROMINI

This tribe is well established in the hobby, although the taxonomy is rather confused. Not only have numerous authorities produced different systems, there are intermediate forms. It simply is not possible to make a diagnosis based on a photograph, which is nevertheless how many aquarium strains were identified. Even worse, many photographs are probably misidentified. In addition, after so long in the hobby, there are aquarium strains that are probably of multiple hybrid origin.

The wide ranges and multiple morphs of several species leave open the possibility that there are even more species than are currently identified. Whatever the final taxonomic resolution of Hemichromini, there are three distinct groups: the (for now) monotypic genus *Anomalochromis*, and in the genus *Hemichromis* the five-spots and the jewel cichlids.

Natural History & Aquarium Husbandry

Interestingly, these fish suffer from time-displaced bad press. In the early days of the hobby, when poeciliids were standard and *Pterophyllum* was the most common cichlid, the jewel cichlids *Hemichromis* spp. were labeled as vicious. And, indeed, putting a male and a female into a 10-gallon tank is an easy recipe for disaster. These fish, however, are no different from hundreds of cichlid species, and properly maintained and managed, they are wonderful aquarium fish. In fact, some are downright shy compared to other cichlids.

Hemichromines are usually easy to breed. All species are pair-bonding, open substrate spawners, and both parents usually take equal care of the eggs and fry. In some species it is more common for the female to tend the brood while the male patrols the territory. Unusually for cichlids, *Hemichromis* fry are often too small for brine shrimp nauplii, and smaller foods must be offered at first.

Anomalochromis thomasi
GREENWOOD 1985

| 6.8 | 7.0 | 7.2 |

Size: 2.75 inches (7 cm) TL.

Dietary Notes: Omnivorous.

Remarks: Two rather distinct morphs exist in the hobby, one from Guinea, the other from Sierra Leone. Appearing as washed-out but still very colorful versions of *Hemichromis* jewels, the most distinguishing characteristic between the two genera is the coloration of the fry—black and white spotted in *Anomalochromis*, brown with black lateral stripes in all *Hemichromis*. Unlike the *Hemichromis*, this species requires soft, neutral water for successful breeding.

Hemichromis bimaculatus
GILL 1862

6.8	7.0	7.2

Trade Names: Jewel cichlid.

Size: 2.75 inches (7 cm) TL.

Dietary Notes: Omnivorous.

Remarks: This is the "original jewel cichlid, but in most cases the name is misused. There are several very similar species in this genus. Someone observing a pair of these cichlids when they decide to spawn will find it hard to believe the transformation of a pinkish-green fish with iridescent blue spangles into a blood-red animal with those contrasting blue jewel-spots.

Hemichromis elongatus
(GUICHENOT 1861)

Trade Names: Five-spot jewel cichlid.

Size: 10 inches (25 cm) TL.

Dietary Notes: A predator, especially of small fishes.

Remarks: These cichlids maintain their black spots, even when in spawning coloration, in which intense red appears on the head and belly. Much larger than the jewels, the species in this genus require appropriately larger accommodations.

Hemichromis fasciatus
PETERS 1858

Trade Names: Five-spot jewel cichlid.

Size: 10 inches (25 cm) TL.

Dietary Notes: A predator, especially of small fishes.

Remarks: This species can be distinguished from other two five-spot species (*elongatus* and *frempongi*) by the presence of small black dots on the anterior of the body, so numerous that they may merge into black blotches. The black spots on the sides may be elongated into partial bars.

LAMPROLOGINI

Although this tribe is famously associated with Lake Tanganyika, a handful of species in one genus inhabit the Congo River drainage, including the type species *Lamprologus congoensis*. These are all rheophilic cichlids, resembling *Steatocranus* or *Teleogramma* in form and behavior. They have an elongate shape and a reduced swim bladder, and they inhabit rapids, living in caves among rocks. All are rather drab, and the only dimorphism they display is size—females are about two-thirds the size of males. Old males can develop a nuchal hump.

Natural History & Aquarium Husbandry

Since they come from rapids, oxygenation is of prime concern in a riverine lamprologine tank. A powerhead placed at one end, aimed down the length of the tank, is always a good setup for rheophilic species of any kind, from native darters to African reophilic cichlids. As these fish are quite territorial and aggressive, large tanks with plenty of hiding caves are required. Their natural diet is small crustaceans and other invertebrates, so they are well cared for by a carnivorous diet in captivity.

Lamprologus congoensis is the type species for the tribe Lamprologini.

Lamprologus congoensis
SCHILTHUIS 1891

| 6.8 | 7.0 | 7.2 |

Size: 6 inches (15 cm) TL.

Dietary Notes: A micropredator.

Remarks: The only species in this group that is regularly available in the hobby. It pales against the lamps from Tanganyika, but it is an interesting and unusual cichlid that appeals to specialists.

Lamprologus lethops
ROBERTS & STEWART 1976

6.8	7.0	7.2

Size: 4 inches (10 cm) TL.

Dietary Notes: Possibly a snail eater.

Remarks: You are not likely to encounter this extremely rare fish, known only from two preserved specimens. It merits mention, though, as the only blind cichlid. It is completely cryptophthalmic, its vestigial eyes buried under tissue. It is also pale in color, suggesting the species might actually be a cavern dweller. Perhaps some undiscovered subterranean river is full of these elusive fish.

PELMATOCHROMINI

There is a lot of history to this taxon. The genus *Pelmatochromis* was for a long time a catchall genus, and more than 50 West African pseudocrenilabrines were assigned to it. Today fewer than half a dozen cichlids are in the genus, and only one in the other pelmatochromine genus, *Pterochromis*. That fish, *Pterochromis congicus*, is unknown in the hobby.

Natural History & Aquarium Husbandry

Its species have no flamboyant colors, and they are medium large at 6 to 10 inches (15 to 25 cm), but there are many popular cichlids that are quite similar, so perhaps they might some day find a following among aquarists. They are for the most part peaceful in the aquarium.

Pelmatochromis buettikoferi
(STEINDACHNER 1894)

Size: 10 inches (25 cm) TL.

Dietary Notes: An omnivore.

Remarks: A large dark spot on the back below the dorsal fin is characteristic of this species. A red belly and some blue and red spots in the fins give this fish a bit of color.

UNAFFILIATED GENUS

The recent discovery of the genus *Etia*, so far monotypic, has provided the hobby with a truly unusual cichlid. Its distinctive concave dorsal fin and large post-pectoral bar or blotch provide interest in an otherwise drab fish. It has affinities with the basal Heterochromidae and Tylochromini but otherwise cannot be easily placed within African Cichlidae.

Etia nguti
SCHLIEWEN & STASSNY 2003

Size: 8 inches (20 cm) TL.

Dietary Notes: A detritivore.

Remarks: Available right after its discovery, this fish has not yet become established in the hobby. High intraspecific aggression requires a large tank with plenty of hiding places. This fish is a larvophilic maternal (usually) mouthbrooder.

West African Tilapiini

Since this is a very large, apparently polyphyletic group, it is not surprising that its members cover quite a range of forms and behaviors. There are true dwarfs like *Tilapia snyderae* and giants like the 16-inch *T. buttikoferi*. Due to the great diversity in this tribe, we will subdivide it by genus, and their natural history and aquarium husbandry will be covered at the generic level.

Traditionally, any fish in this tribe might be called a "tilapia," no matter what its genus. To further complicate things, that name comes from a native African word that applies to a specific type of fish, without regard to taxonomic concerns, yet it probably doesn't apply to all the fish called tilapia by scientists.

CHILOCHROMIS

A monotypic genus. Like many West African cichlids, body shape is somewhat variable, being longer in specimens from fast-flowing water and more high bodied in fish from more lentic habitats.

This cichlid is a large, aggressive, monomorphic, substrate spawner. Obviously, then, it requires very large aquaria and typical large cichlid maintenance. Despite its century of being known to science, it is not really known in the hobby.

GOBIOCICHLA

As the name implies, fish of this genus are goby-like, adapted for a benthic lifestyle in rapids. Convergent evolution has produced similar cichlids in several groups. This genus and *Steatocranus* are the tilapiine examples.

Gobiocichla wonderi
KANAZAWA 1951

| 6.8 | 7.0 | 7.2 |

Size: 4.75 inches (12 cm) TL.

Dietary Notes: Primarily herbivorous.

Remarks: This species and its congener *G. ethelwynnae* are rapids dwellers with extremely elongated bodies, reduced swim bladders, and single lateral lines. They are cave spawners and are very aggressive when breeding.

A demand for high oxygenation and plenty of floorspace are the typical requirements of goby-like cichlids, along with plenty of rocks and caves.

OREOCHROMIS

This genus has about three dozen species, one dozen of which live in West and Central Africa. The *Oreochromis* are closely related to both *Sarotherodon* and *Tilapia*. These medium to large cichlids are typically prolific and highly adaptable. The fish grow quickly and spawn at an early age. They can survive in fresh or brackish conditions. They are also extremely tasty. This makes them an ideal human food source, and they have been widely introduced around the world. Unfortunately, because they are prolific and highly adaptable and have been widely introduced, this has spelled disaster for many ecosystems around the world.

Hybrids (usually *O. aureus* x *O. mossambicus* or *O. niloticus* x *O. mossambicus*) have been developed for the aquaculture trade, and a red morph, which is extremely popular for market purposes, has also become common in the hobby.

Natural History & Aquarium Husbandry

Not widely available, the cichlids of this genus are available occasionally and make good aquarium specimens for large tanks. Although opportunistically omnivorous, these cichlids are primarily herbivorous, feeding on phytoplankton, algae, and vegetation. If kept in large aquaria they are easy to keep and breed. Most species are quite gregarious, and it is even possible to find males' spawning pits close to each other in the wild.

In the larger species, females may spawn between 1000 and 2000 eggs in clutches of about 100. Subsequent clutches may be fertilized by different males. The fry are first released about two weeks after spawning and may remain with the mother for another week.

Oreochromis macrochir
(BOULENGER 1912)

| 6.8 | 7.0 | 7.2 |

Size: 12 inches (30 cm) TL.

Dietary Notes: Primarily herbivorous.

Remarks: This cichlid has been in the hobby a long time, though currently it is not very popular. It is one of the species in which the male has an elaborate genital papilla or "tassel," at which the female pecks during spawning to ensure fertilization of the eggs.

Oreochromis mossambicus
(PETERS 1852)

Size: 12 inches (30 cm) TL.

Dietary Notes: Primarily herbivorous.

Remarks: This may be the most adaptable of the group, surviving temperatures from 50° to 95°F (10° to 35°C) and salinities from fresh to full marine. It is probably the most widely introduced tilapia, reported established in Africa, Asia, and the Americas.

STEATOCRANUS

This unusual genus contains about 10 species of rheophilic, bottom-hugging, cave-spawning cichlids with reduced swim bladders and an elongate and compressed form. Basically grey, they have a subtle beauty that is well balanced by their intriguing personality and behavior.

Natural History & Aquarium Husbandry

As with most goby-like cichlids, these fish need plenty of room on the floor of the aquarium, as well as high oxygen levels and pristine water conditions. A powerhead setup is best, with plenty of large water changes. Provide a lot of rocks so there are many hiding places.

Although *Steatocranus gibbiceps* appears to be primarily a molluscivore, all species will take regular aquarium fare in captivity. They breed readily, and as the male protects his territory rather than a brood, multiple broods can be raised in one tank. The female cares for the eggs and fry in a cave. The fry stick quite close to the cave for a long time and are not typically led about the tank by their parents.

Despite their bulldog appearance, these fish are peaceful and can be kept in a community tank that does not include direct competitors for the bottom real estate.

A pair of *Steatocranus tinanti* peeks from their hiding place.

Steatocranus casuarius
POLL 1939

6.8	7.0	7.2

TradeNames: Buffalo-head cichlid.

Size: 4.75 inches (12 cm) TL.

Dietary Notes: Feeds primarily on algae.

Remarks: The most common species in the hobby, this fish is found in open water much more often than its congeners, which stick to the rapids. Both sexes have a hump on the head, with the male's being much larger.

Steatocranus irvinei
(TREWAVAS 1943)

Size: 6.75 inches (17 cm) TL.

Dietary Notes: Feeds primarily on algae.

Remarks: Moved from the genus *Gobiochromis* in 1976, this blue-lipped species is markedly different from its current congeners: larger, more slender, less benthic, more aggressive, more active in parenting by both parents. It is also the only species in the genus not found in the Congo system. Whether it remains in this genus or not remains to be determined.

Steatocranus tinanti
(POLL 1939)

| 6.8 | 7.0 | 7.2 |

Size: 6 inches (15 cm) TL.

Dietary Notes: Feeds primarily on algae.

Remarks: Fairly common in the hobby, this very slender cichlids shows marked sexual dimorphism, with males developing a massive head and hump.

TILAPIA

If subsequent research upholds the finding that this genus is monotypic with just the type species *T. sparrmanii*, there will be about 40 species orphaned. The half-dozen recognized subspecies will certainly come into focus at that time. These cichlids are widespread and diverse. Many are quite colorful, and they are beginning to be offered more often in the trade. They are similar in size, temperament, and behavior to many Central American cichlids and are increasingly being "discovered" by cichlasomine fans.

Natural History & Aquarium Husbandry

For the most part, these species are herbivores, feeding primarily on aquatic plants. They should receive a diet based on vegetable foods. All are substrate spawners, though some species prefer a sheltered location rather than an open area to deposit the spawn. A few—notably Lake Bermin—species are actually cave spawners.

The brilliant red eye of *Tilapia mariae* is a feature that makes this species very attractive to hobbyists.

Tilapia brevimanus
Boulenger 1911
Size: 8.5 inches (22 cm) TL.

Tilapia busumana
(Guenther 1903)
Size: 10 inches (25 cm) TL.

Tilapia guineensis
(Bleeker 1862)
Size: 10 inches (25 cm) TL.

Tilapia joka
Thys van den Audenaerde 1969
Size: 6 inches (15 cm) TL.

Tilapia mariae
Boulenger 1899
Size: 14 inches (35 cm) TL.

Tilapia zilli
Gervais 1848
Size: 12 inches (30 cm) TL.

Please see remarks opposite
regarding care and husbandry.

Tilapia buttikoferi
(HUBRECHT 1881)

Size: 16 inches (40 cm) TL.

Dietary Notes: Primarily herbivorous.

Remarks: This fish is widespread in the hobby. Its striking barred coloration and high, laterally compressed body shape appeal to many fans of very large and aggressive cichlids. Once established, the pair bond is strong, and you can expect a great many offspring.

Chapter 8

Region 6 South America

We now begin the last leg of our journey through the world's cichlids. We've already covered the living fossils of Madagascar and Asia, and we've plowed through the incredible radiation of Cichlidae in four different regions in Africa. In doing this we've followed the chronological, evolutionary, and biogeographical history of cichlids in the Old World. There remains, however, another incredible cichlid story that was taking place halfway across the world.

AN IRONY

While Africa was largely unexplored, much study was going on the other side of the world, where Europe's conquest and colonization had an earlier start. Consequently, we wound up with the family Cichlidae, its type species being in the genus *Cichla*, the only genus in the tribe Cichlini. Thus, the subfamily Cichlinae, which at one time contained all but one of the dozen or so American tribes, takes its name from a very small group of fishes.

Cichla monoculus
Spix & Agassiz 1831
Size: 24 inches (60 cm) TL.

Cichla orinocensis
Humboldt 1821
Size: 30 inches (75 cm) TL.

Cichla temensis
Humboldt 1821
Size: 30 inches (75 cm) TL.

***Cichla* sp. "Xingu"**
Size: Probably more than 20
inches (50 cm) TL.

Cichla ocellaris
Bloch & Schneider 1801
Size: 24 inches (60 cm) TL.

Cichla orinocensis
Humboldt 1821
Size: 30 inches (75 cm) TL.

Please see remarks opposite
regarding care and husbandry.

Natural History & Captive Husbandry

Since the smallest of the genus *(Cichla intermedia)* grows to nearly 24 inches (60 cm) in length, they should be afforded the largest possible aquaria to live in. All *Cichla* are piscivorous by nature and should be cared for accordingly. Captive-raised specimens can often be transferred to non-living foods, like pellets and smelt for example, with some ease. Careful attention should be paid to water quality, as *Cichla* will rapidly show signs of head-and-lateral-line erosion if metabolites are allowed to build up.

Cichla ocellaris
BLOCH & SCHNEIDER 1801

6.6	6.8	7.0

Trade Name: Butterfly peacock bass.

Size: 24 inches (60 cm) TL.

Dietary Notes: A piscivore.

Remarks: Native to northeastern Brazil, Guyana, and Surinam, adults of this species are distinguishable by their glaring red eyes and single spot where the third vertical bar was as a juvenile. Unfortunately, juveniles and sub-adults are very similar in appearance to *C. monoculus* to the south and *C. orinocensis* to the west.

Cichla orinocensis is a popular aquarium resident.

CRENICICHLINI

Two genera make up this tribe, the pike cichlids, with about 80 described species in *Crenicichla* and seven in *Teleocichla*. Although pike cichlids are generally thought of being large fish—and many are!—there are some very small species which could certainly be called dwarfs. This is yet another group of cichlids in which the females are generally more colorful than the males.

Natural History & Aquarium Husbandry

Those dwarfs need decent-sized tanks, and the larger pikes need very large aquaria. They should be maintained in nothing but the largest aquariums and kept in clean, clear water that is filtered over peat for best results. A pair of pikes can usually be kept together as long as plenty of hiding spots and visual barriers are present to divide up the tank.

Although not as large as *Cichla*, pike cichlids are largely piscivorous; they simply eat smaller fish. Even the tiny species *Crenicichla compressiceps* feeds principally on the fry of other cichlids. They will, of course, consume invertebrates they come across, and with patience they all should be able to be trained to non living foods.

Breeding success with these crenicichlines is uncommon enough that only master breeders have reported it. It is quite likely that once tank-bred specimens become widespread in the hobby, more people will be breeding these species.

Nearly all species of jumbo pike cichlids will show signs of head and lateral line erosion should their environment become too polluted. Frequent, large-scale water changes, along with a good and varied diet, will help prevent this disorder from happening.

Crenicichla acutirostris
Günther 1862
Size: 12 inches (30 cm) TL.

Crenicichla cincta
Regan 1905
Size: 16 inches (40 cm) TL.

Crenicichla compressiceps
Ploeg 1986
Size: 4 inches (10 cm) TL;
usually slightly smaller.

Crenicichla geayi
Pellegrin 1903
Size: 8 inches (20 cm) TL.

Crenicichla johanna
Heckel 1840
Size: 16 inches (40 cm) TL.

Crenicichla lenticulata
Heckel 1840
Size: 16 inches (40 cm) TL.

Please see remarks opposite
regarding care and husbandry.

Crenicichla jegui
PLOEG 1986

| 6.6 | 6.8 | 7.0 |

Trade Names: Pike cichlid.

Size: 8 inches (20 cm) TL, sometimes larger.

Dietary Notes: A piscivore.

Remarks: This interesting fish from northern Brazil is a bottom-dwelling species that lives in submerged structures such as roots and branches. They are a sedentary species that will only move if provoked or when food is placed in their tank. They are somewhat intolerant of each other, and there are no published accounts of captive breeding.

Crenicichla lepidota
HECKEL 1840

Trade Name: Pike cichlid.

Size: 4 inches (10 cm) TL; may grow slightly larger.

Dietary Notes: A piscivore.

Remarks: This species from Brazil is one of the original pike cichlids; the species is one of the oldest and most widely available species of pike cichlids that hobbyists are likely to come in contact with.

Crenicichla lugubris
HECKEL 1840

6.6	6.8	7.0

Trade Name: Pike cichlid.

Size: 16 inches (40 cm) TL; usually smaller.

Dietary Notes: A piscivore.

Remarks: There are many color varieties of *C. lugubris*. Some appear striated, especially as juveniles, while others exhibit large red to green blotches randomly spread over their bodies. Such color variability is generally related to the fish's diet or possibly even the water chemistry of the area they live.

Crenicichla missioneira
Lucena & Kullander 1992
Size: 8 inches (20 cm) TL.

Crenicichla macrophthalma
Heckel 1840
Size: 10 inches (25 cm) TL.

Crenicichla notophthalmus
Regan 1913
Size: 6 inches (15 cm) TL.

Crenicichla percna
Kullander 1991
Size: 14 inches (35 cm) TL.

Crenicichla regani
Ploeg 1989
Size: 4 inches (10 cm) TL.

Crenicichla saxatilis
Linnaeus 1758
Size: 8 inches (20 cm) TL.

Please see remarks opposite
for additional information.

Crenicichla marmorata
PELLEGRIN 1904

6.6	6.8	7.0

21.1 26.6 32.2 37.7 °C
70 80 90 100 °F

Trade Name: Pike cichlid.
Size: 14 inches (35 cm) TL.
Dietary Notes: A piscivore.
Remarks: This pike from the Rio Tapajós is most easily distinguished eight to nine light pink to reddish-orange blotches that run horizontally down the flanks. The underside of the female is pink, while the male's underside remains a somewhat dull cream. Juveniles go through dramatic color transformations and are difficult to identify.

269

***Crenicichla* sp. "cobra"**
Size: Greater than 12 inches (30 cm) TL.

***Crenicichla* sp. "Tapajós Red"**
Size: Estimated at 12 inches (30 cm) TL.

***Crenicichla* sp. "Xingu I"**
Size: Estimated at more than 12 inches (30 cm) TL.

***Crenicichla* sp. "Xingu II"**
Size: Estimated at more than 12 inches (30 cm) TL.

***Crenicichla* sp. "Xingu III"**
Size: Estimated at more than 12 inches (30 cm) TL.

Crenicichla gaucho
Lucena & Kullander 1992
Size: 6 inches (15 cm) TL.

Please see remarks opposite regarding care and husbandry.

Crenicichla strigata
GUENTHER 1862

Trade Name: Striated pike cichlid.

Size: 14 inches (35 cm) TL.

Dietary Notes: A piscivore.

Remarks: Distributed over a wide area in Brazil, this might represent a species complex. All pike cichlids are predators, but not all grow to a huge size, like those of the strigata complex. Their care and husbandry in aquariums is basic, however. Clean, warm water of a moderate hardness is a good start. Since many species within the genus are sensitive to cephalic erosion of their neuromast pores, it's a good idea to perform large water changes on a regular basis.

Crenicichla vittataa
Heckel 1840

Size: 14 inches (35 cm) TL.

Trade Name: Vittatus pike cichlid.

Dietary Notes: A piscivore.

Remarks: Another species where the males are more brilliantly colored than the females. This species from Argentina and Paraguay is a cool water cichlid.

Teleocichla cinderella
KULLANDER 1988

Size: 3.5 inches (9 cm) TL.

Dietary Notes: A predator.

Remarks: These dwarfs from the Rio Tocantins require excellent water quality and some current, as they are primarily found in the faster moving shallow waters of rivers and tributaries throughout their range.

Astronotinae
&
Cichlasomatinae

ASTRONOTINAE

This subfamily comprises two tribes, each with a single genus. All the species are primitive cichlids, and many consider them basal for the South American clade. There is some disagreement on grouping these two tribes, but, despite their considerable differences, they appear to be closely related.

Astronotini

The oscar has been popular for decades, bred so long in captivity that there are a dozen or more domesticated strains, including long finned and various color forms. For most of that time, the fish was known as *Astronotus ocellatus*. Another species, *A. crassipinnis*, was recognized but was rarely imported. A third, *A. orbiculatus*, is considered valid by some. These fishes are highly variable across a large range, so more species may be forthcoming. The origin of the domesticated oscar is uncertain and suspected to be hybrid. Currently imported oscars are often designated by locale, so serious breeders can keep them separate.

Natural History & Aquarium Husbandry

These fishes are widespread in the Amazon, and the common oscar is firmly established as an alien invader in Florida, where it is enjoyed as a game fish popular both for its fighting spirit and for its excellent flavor.

Although very hardy and long-lived when properly maintained, this fish is often mistreated. Frequent large water changes are necessary to prevent head and lateral line erosion (HLLE). Other than that, their major needs are psychological—as intelligent animals they need distraction. Many enjoy playing with floating plastic plants, rubber balls, or other toys. If given gravel—problematic for maintaining these messy, heavy feeders—they will enjoy bulldozing it to fit their constantly changing aesthetics. Figure a minimum of 20 to 50 gallons of tankspace per oscar. For cichlids, oscars are rather mild and typically get along with other less-belligerent cichlids and with large non-cichlids. Of course, territoriality and spawning readiness can challenge even long-term peace.

These fish are largely carnivorous, but as much of the diet is small invertebrates, a lot of vegetable matter is consumed in the guts of the prey items. The worst food is feeder fish, which have killed and maimed many a pet oscar through disease and dietary deficiency. Oscars consume any foods greedily, and there is no need to use live foods.

Although experts can vent sex these fish, the sexes are otherwise indistinguishable. Best results are obtained in any case with pairs that form naturally. They breed in typical substrate-spawning cichlid fashion, with large spawns, and are excellent parents. Obviously, a large aquarium is necessary. Pairs are usually stable and reliable spawners, especially compared to many other large cichlids, but as with any cichlid, unfortunate things happen occasionally.

Astronotus crassipinnis
(HECKEL 1840)

6.6	6.8	7.0

Size: 15 inches to 18 inches (40 to 46 cm) TL.

Dietary Notes: A predator that relishes insects.

Remarks: This species is supposed to have a tiger-type pattern on a bland and very drab background. This oscar species is capable of surviving, and even thriving, in cooler-than-normal water, as they're exposed to temperatures in the 60sF on a regular basis throughout their natural range. Even still, an aquarium in the normal tropical range is advised.

Astronotus ocellatus
(AGASSIZ 1831)

Size: 15 inches to 18 inches (40 to 46 cm) TL.

Dietary Notes: A predator that relishes insects.

Remarks: Aside from the angelfish *Pterophyllum scalare*, the oscar is by far the most popular and easily recognized species of cichlid. They make great pets and are rather unaggressive for such a large cichlid.

Chaetobranchini

In contrast to the popular oscar, which even many non aquarists recognize, the chaetobranchines are not at all well known in the hobby. There are two genera, each with two recognized species. Some have never been imported, and none are commonly available. They have had a bit more popularity in Europe, but even there they have never been successfully bred.

Natural History & Aquarium Husbandry

These extremely challenging cichlids are plankton feeders. They have highly protrusible mouths that earn them the name "basketmouths." This trait has developed convergently in the basketmouths of the genus *Acaronia*, which are sometimes called "true basketmouths," while the chaetobranchines are "false basketmouths" (a name shared with fish of the genus *Caquetaia* as well). Since there is no such thing as a correct common name—or an incorrect one for that matter!—this is pseudo accuracy and only serves to mislead people.

The other basketmouths use their impressive maw to suck in other fishes. The chaetobranchines use theirs as part of an oral pump, sucking in plankton-rich water and pumping it over their elaborate gill rakers, which strain out the edible bits and send the waste water out the opercula.

Obviously, then, feeding is a major challenge with these fish. Some extremely dedicated aquarists have managed to maintain these large cichlids with copious quantities of live brine shrimp nauplii and daphnia, but the fish typically starve in captivity. A few aquarists have gotten them to eat pellets and other more usual fare, and such fish are likely to be the first spawned.

Chaetobranchus flavescens
HECKEL 1840

HECKEL 1840

Size: 8.25 inches (21 cm) TL.

Dietary Notes: A planktonivore.

Remarks: This basketmouth is widespread throughout northern South America.

CICHLASOMATINAE

Created in the fallout of the dissolution of *Cichlasoma*, this subfamily comprises three tribes, Acaroniini, Cichlasomatini, and Heroini.

Acaroniini

This small tribe contains two cichlids that superficially resemble Chaetobranchini.

Acaronia nassa
(HECKEL 1840)

6.6	6.8	7.0

Trade Name: Basketmouth.

Size: 10 inches (25 cm) TL.

Dietary Notes: A predator.

Remarks: The original and for a long time only basketmouth species, this fish is widespread in the Amazon drainage.

These fish are predators, using their basket-like protrusible mouths to engulf and inhale invertebrates and small fishes. They have large eyes and are adapted to hunting in dim light.

Cichlasomatini

The cichlasomines used to include what is now considered the cichlasomatines and the heroines. In the aftermath of the first systematic reorganizations of these fishes, when the dozens of *"Cichlasoma"* and *"Aequidens"* species were divided out into other genera, when some taxonomists dumped the many North American orphans into *"Herichthys,"* it is sometimes difficult to remember that there are still plenty of valid *Aequidens*, *Cichlasoma*, and *Herichthys* species. The South Americans of the tribe Cichlasomatini are the acaras, many of which have been popular aquarium specimens for many years. The genus *Cichlasoma* is now restricted to the dozen various port cichlids in South America, some of which are long-term favorites. They are all so similar it is difficult to tell them apart, and many species have been imported as ports, labeled either *Aequidens portalegrensis* or *Cichlasoma portalegrense*.

The *Aequidens* complex contains many species that are in of further study.

Aequidens is also restricted now to about a dozen species, closely related to *Cichlasoma*, though often more colorful. Included in this orphanage with the green terrors are the blue acaras, the former including the only acaras on the Pacific side of the Andes, the latter including the only acaras from North America (Panama and Costa Rica).

Natural History & Aquarium Husbandry

There is considerable variability in this group, but most are mid-size cichlids of moderate aggressiveness. As the common name suggests, the species known as inchesgreen terrors inches are the most aggressive of the group, though compared to North American *guapote* or African tropheines, they are pussycats. Most other cichlasomatine species are extremely mild mannered cichlids.

As it can be difficult to tell the acara species apart, for breeding purposes it is best to get specimens of known origin. Those with broad ranges are typically found in various habitats. Species with more restricted ranges may be more demanding as to water chemistry, especially for spawning. Almost all of these fishes are substrate spawners; they usually choose a flat rock for their eggs. Both parents tend the eggs and the fry. A few species do practice mouthbrooding.

For the most part, all of these cichlids are opportunistic omnivores and will do well with standard aquarium fare. Meaty foods with occasional plant matter make a fine diet. As many of these species come from southern South America, including Uruguay and Argentina, they are accustomed to cooler water than most other cichlids and may do fine in unheated tanks. When in doubt as to the natural range of your fish, however, it is best to treat them as tropical.

Aequidens sp. "gold saum" is not the real green terror.
It's a closely related species that remains undescribed
at time of this publication.

Aequidens diadema
(Heckel 1840)
Size: 4.75 inches (12 cm) TL.

Aequidens hoehnei
(Miranda-Ribeiro 1918)
Size: 4.75 inches (12 cm) TL.

Aequidens metae
Eigenmann 1922
Size: 5 inches (13 cm) TL.

Aequidens patricki
Kullander 1984
Size: 6 inches (15 cm) TL.

Aequidens patricki
Kullander 1984
Size: 6 inches (15 cm) TL.

"Aequidens" latifrons
(Steindachner 1878)
Size: 6 inches (15 cm) TL.

Please see remarks opposite
regarding care and husbandry.

"Aequidens" pulcher
(GILL 1858)

Trade Name: Blue acara.

Size: 6 inches (15 cm) TL.

Dietary Notes: An omnivore.

Remarks: This is the original blue acara, from northern Venezuela and Trinidad. It is an excellent beginner's cichlid. Just like the species on the previous page, the blue acara is a dedicated parent and guardian of their spawn. Often, males will defend a territory while the females tend to the eggs and brood. A warm, dimly lit aquarium with plenty of hiding places makes for a perfect habitat for members of this group.

"Aequidens" sapayensis
(Regan 1903)
Size: 6 inches (15 cm) TL.

"Aequidens" sp. "gold saum"
Undescribed to Date
Size: 10 inches (25 cm) TL.

"Aequidens" sp. "silver saum"
Undescribed to Date
Size: 10 inches (25 cm) TL.

"Aequidens" rivulatus
(Günther 1859)
Size: 8 inches (20 cm) TL.

"Aequidens" pulcher
(Gill 1858)
Size: 6 inches (15 cm) TL.

"Aequidens" sp. "gold saum"
Undescribed to Date
Size: 10 inches (25 cm) TL.

Please see remarks opposite
regarding care and husbandry.

"Aequidens" rivulatus
(GÜNTHER 1859)

6.6	6.8	7.0

21.1 26.6 32.2 37.7 °C
70   80   90   100 °F

Trade Name: Green Terror
(GÜNTHER 1859)
Size: 8 inches (20 cm) TL.
Dietary Notes: An omnivore.
Remarks: Only recently has this species become available to hobbyists after many, many years of being absent. Most green terrors in the hobby are undescribed *"Aequidens"* species. All species, however, have the same basic care and husbandry requirements in aquariums. Warm, dimly lit aquariums with plenty of hiding places and visual barriers make for a perfect environment. While able to be kept in a community with other large fishes, members of *"Aequidens"* should not be housed with others of the same group, as there seems to be a high degree of intra-specific squabbling that goes on. This may even be the case in very large aquaria, too.

"Aequidens" sp. **"silver saum"**
UNDESCRIBED TO DATE

6.6	6.8	7.0

Trade Name: Green terror.

Size: 10 inches (25 cm) TL.

Dietary Notes: An omnivore.

Remarks: Another to-be-described species in this complex. Sometime also referred to as the "silver seam" terror, this species has the exact same care and husbandry requirements as others of the genus.

Bujurquina mariae
(EIGENMANN 1922)

| 6.6 | 6.8 | 7.0 |

Size: 6 inches (15 cm) TL.

Dietary Notes: An omnivore.

Remarks: These highly underestimated cichlids are not very common in the hobby, and that is unfortunate, since mature specimens in good health are gorgeously colored. Of the 17 described species in the genus, only a couple are usually available, and those not readily.

Bujurquina vittata
(HECKEL 1840)

Size: 4.75 inches (12 cm) TL.

Dietary Notes: An omnivore.

Remarks: Bolivia holds many treasures that are unknown to the aquarium hobby. This species is one of them. Sure to gain popularity as time progresses, *B. vittata* is already seeing a following in certain areas where fishes from Bolivia are being exported regularly.

Cichlasoma portalegrense
(HENSEL 1870)

6.6	6.8	7.0

Size: 4 inches (10 cm) TL.

Dietary Notes: An omnivore.

Remarks: The original port cichlid popular for decades, though other species have been imported under this name.

Cichlasoma amazonarum
Kullander 1983
Size: 4 inches (10 cm) TL.

Cichlasoma bimaculatum
(Linnaeus 1758)
Size: 6 inches (15 cm) TL.

Cichlasoma boliviense
Kullander 1983
Size: 4.5 inches (11 cm) TL.

Cichlasoma dimerus
(Heckel 1840)
Size: 5 inches (12 cm) TL.

***Cichlasoma* sp.**
Undescribed to Date
Size: 5 inches (12 cm) TL.

Cichlasoma bimaculatum
(Linnaeus 1758)
Size: 6 inches (15 cm) TL.

Please see remarks opposite regarding care and husbandry.

Cleithracara maroni
(STEINDACHNER 1881)

6.6	6.8	7.0

Trade Name: Keyhole cichlid.

Size: 6 inches (15 cm) TL.

Dietary Notes: An omnivore.

Remarks: A monotypic genus, and a peaceful species. Many years ago there were very few cichlid species available, and this was one of them. All *Cichlasoma*-types are easily cared for in home aquariums. Provide a warm, dimly lit aquarium that has plenty of hiding places. Community aquariums are fine, usually, as long as their tankmates cannot easily be swallowed. Members of this group seem to prefer small crustaceans and some plant material as their primary food sources.

Krobia guianensis
(REGAN 1905)

6.6	6.8	7.0

Size: 8 inches (20 cm) TL.

Dietary Notes: An omnivore.

Remarks: This interesting cichlid from Guyana does not ship well and are often in poor condition upon arrival. After they are properly adjusted, they prove to be a tough and hardy species. There are a few other species in the genus, some yet to be described.

Laetacara dorsigera
(HECKEL 1840)

| 6.6 | 6.8 | 7.0 |

Size: 4 inches (10 cm) TL.

Dietary Notes: An omnivore.

Remarks: Just like *L. curviceps*, this species does well in a community aquarium with other peaceful fishes with similar habits, but *L. dorsigerus* prefers slightly cooler water.

Laetacara thayeri
(STEINDACHNERI 1875)

  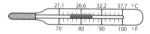

Size: 5 inches (12 cm) TL.
Dietary Notes: An omnivore.
Remarks: This is the larger cousin to the ever-popular *L. curviceps*. It is gaining in popularity among specialists.

Nannacara adoketa
KULLANDER & PRADA-PEDREROS 1993

Size: 4 inches (10 cm) TL.

Dietary Notes: Feeds primarily on small invertebrates.

Remarks: This newly available species may be assigned to a new genus eventually. While not overly colorful, *N. adoketa* are a nice addition to the community aquarium, as they are quite peaceful.

Nannacara anomala
REGAN 1905

6.6	6.8	7.0

Size: 3 inches (7.5 cm) TL.

Dietary Notes: Feeds primarily on small invertebrates.

Remarks: This long-time favorite dwarf cichlid can be harem spawned with one male and several females in a large aquarium. Like the other half-dozen species in this genus, it is generally peaceful, except when spawning.

Tahuantinsuyoa macantzatza
KULLANDER 1986

6.6	6.8	7.0

Size: 4.75 inches (12 cm) TL.

Dietary Notes: An omnivore.

Remarks: A softwater species from the Rio Aguaytía. This species is just becoming popular with hobbyists, despite it being present in the hobby for more than a decade now. Many keepers report this fish as able to be kept in a community with other similar-sized fishes.

Heroini

We will revisit this tribe again in our next—and last—region, North America, as it is heroines that invaded the northern landmass when a land bridge appeared at the Isthmus of Panama and radiated to fill niches all the way up into Texas. It still contains, however, about 40 species in South America, many of them long-time favorites.

Most of these species are high bodied and laterally compressed. They are typically very peaceful, especially for large cichlids. Ironically, the most aggressive cichlids in this hemisphere, the Central American *guapotes*, are also heroines. The evolutionarily rapid plasticity of cichlids is also apparent in that while many of the South American heroines are fully adapted to very soft, acid water, the North American species are adapted to hard, basic water and even brackish conditions.

Taxonomic Issues

Of course there is much work still to be done among the heroines, with new species certain to be described and further refinements to be made. There are several current issues of particular note:

Leftover Orphans

The ongoing restructuring of South American cichlid taxonomies leaves us currently with two orphaned groups in this tribe, both leftover *"Cichlasoma."* One is the *"Cichlasoma" facetum* group, with three species: *facetum*, *tembe*, and *scitulum*. The other contains a few other species that are considered heroines but are not in that group—in other words, non port cichlid, non *facetum*, ex-*Cichlasoma*.

The orphans are listed here as *"Cichlasoma."* This designation, unfortunately, applies to three disparate groups, all formerly considered in the genus *Cichlasoma*: the *facetum* group, the other South American orphans, and the still unassigned species in Central America, which are themselves certainly a polyphyletic group. In other words, recognize that this designation merely indicates an unassigned genus of heroine cichlid and not any necessary relatedness of one species to another.

ANGEL PROBLEMS

There is considerable confusion among the actual taxonomic standing of the species within *Pterophyllum*. The *scalare* types still cause problems, especially as new forms are found and exported, and as people consulting older texts keep bringing up other species names. Then there are false taxonomies, probably motivated by market concerns. For example, the "Peruvian altums" are clearly not *altum*, though they are a higher-bodied form of *scalare*.

Also, it appears there may be at least three species within the *altum* complex, though today we only recognize one. As more DNA analysis is done, this genus should prove to be very interesting indeed.

DISCUS VARIATION

Certain species of fish have a great genetic propensity for color variation. Two good examples are *Xiphophorus* species and discus. This is apparent both in the many natural color varieties and in the profusion of domesticated strains. Hybridization (of species) and crossbreeding (of natural color varieties) play an important role in the development of these domesticated morphs, along with selective breeding.

Decades ago, the several varieties of wild discus being imported led to several subspecies designations that have not held up to taxonomic scrutiny. It is now apparent that there is enormous variety among wild populations, with almost every tributary sporting its unique strain of discus. Nevertheless, there are only two species in this genus, but if we were to come back in 10,000 years that might no longer be the case.

While the latent genetic ability to produce many color variants clearly varies from species to species, this does not account in itself account for the different morphs. It would be interesting to see some controlled experiments examining whether wild discus of different strains preferentially pick mates of the same variety.

Severum Species

The genus *Heros* is also a bit confused at this point. The salient points are these:

- The common severum was long thought to be *Cichlasoma severum*, now *Heros severus*.
- Most now consider *H. severus* to be a delayed mouthbrooding species with a restricted range, and the common severum to be either *H. appendiculatus* or *H. efasciatus*.
- Others consider the mouthbrooding population to be a variant of the common severum, *H. severus*.
- The status of *H. appendiculatus* is uncertain; some consider it to be synonymous with either *H. efasciatus* or *H. severus*.

Natural History & Aquarium Husbandry

These cichlids are typically quite adaptable concerning water chemistry. Even those often considered to require soft, acid water at least for spawning have been bred in hard, basic water by some aquarists. In addition, many of the old-time favorites, like *Heros severus*, *Pterophyllum scalare*, and *Symphysodon aequifasciata*, are available in strains that have been aquarium bred for so long that they can thrive in just about any normal tap water.

Much more important than pH and conductivity for almost all these species is water *purity*. Commercial breeders, who strive for maximum production, often use flow-through systems or practice daily complete water changes. Discus and angelfish have proved especially responsive to such treatment. The nil concentrations of dissolved metabolites in such a setup can make up for a multitude of less-than-ideal water parameters.

As mentioned, these are among the mildest large cichlids, and they are very popular for cichlid community tanks and for mixed communities with large non cichlid fishes. Non breeding individuals are usually very well behaved, and even spawning pairs usually direct their aggression only toward conspecifics and toward other fish that threaten their brood.

It is best to consider all heroines to be omnivorous. Even the stealth predators of the genus *Pterophyllum* eat considerable vegetable matter, and species like *Uaru* view a planted tank as a swim-in salad bowl.

Caquetaia kraussii
(STEINDACHNER 1879)

6.6	6.8	7.0

21.1 26.6 32.2 37.7 °C
70 80 90 100 °F

Size: 12 inches (30 cm) TL.

Dietary Notes: Primarily a piscivore.

Remarks: The four big, bold species in this genus are from northern South America. They are not for the average hobbyist, as they are temperamental and require excellent water quality. Aggression is highly variable.

Caquetaia myersi
(SCHULTZ 1944)

6.6	6.8	7.0

Size: 12 inches (30 cm) TL.

Dietary Notes: Primarily a piscivore.

Remarks: This is a very beautiful cichlid with gold to chartreuse coloration. Years ago, this species was virtually impossible to obtain, but although prices are still high, they can now be found with little difficulty. Keep with large, peaceful fishes and provide excellent water quality for best results.

Caquetaia spectabilis
(STEINDACHNER 1875)

Size: 12 inches (30 cm) TL.

Dietary Notes: Primarily a piscivore.

Remarks: This beautiful cichlid is rather difficult to keep healthy in aquariums. They need large aquariums with warm, acidic water that is free of excessive bacteria.

Caquetaia umbrifera
(MEEK & HILDEBRAND 1913)

| 6.6 | 6.8 | 7.0 |

Trade Name: Umbie.

Size: 20 inches (50 cm) TL.

Dietary Notes: Primarily a piscivore.

Remarks: This species directly competes with *Parachromis dovii* for the largest *"Cichlasoma"* award. This robust fish is an open-water species that feeds primarily on whole, live fishes and aquatic invertebrates in nature. Their aquariums should be the largest possible, and filtration, circulation, and water changes should be oversized as well.

"Cichlasoma" facetum
(JENYNS 1842)

Trade Name: Chanchito.

Size: 7 inches (18 cm) TL.

Dietary Notes: An omnivore.

Remarks: Larger and more aggressive than most in the genus, this fish was very popular decades ago and is enjoying resurgence in popularity. It can tolerate cool tropical temperatures.

"Cichlasoma" dimerus
(HECKEL 1840)

| 6.6 | 6.8 | 7.0 |

Size: 6 inches (15 cm) TL.

Dietary Notes: An omnivore.

Remarks: This native of Argentina is used to cooler waters than most South American cichlids.

309

Heros appendiculatus
(Castelnau 1855)
Size: 10 inches (25 cm) TL.

Heros efasciatus
Heckel 1840
Size: 10 inches (25 cm) TL.

Heros notatus
Jardine 1843
Size: 12 inches (30 cm) TL.

Heros severus
Heckel 1840
Size: 12 inches (30 cm) TL.

Heros notatus
Jardine 1843
Size: 12 inches (30 cm) TL.

***Heros severus* "gold"**
Heckel 1840
Size: 12 inches (30 cm) TL.

Please see remarks opposite
for additional information.

Heros **sp. "rotkeil"**
Undescribed to Date

6.6	6.8	7.0

Size: 10 inches (25 cm) TL.

Dietary Notes: Omnivorous, needs plant matter in the diet.

Remarks: This new cichlid on the block is highly recognizable with beginners and experienced aquarists alike. They are probably one of the most beautiful *Heros*, with their bright red heads and blue-green spangles. Aquarium care is identical to others in the genus. Warm, large aquariums that are dimly lit and have bogwood or other types of visual barriers make for a perfect environment. Additionally, these fishes as a whole tend to be somewhat susceptible to head and lateral line erosion, so their water must be kept clean and very fresh. Frequent water changes are a must for members of this group.

Hoplarchus psittacus
(HECKEL 1840)

6.6	6.8	7.0

Trade Name: Parrot cichlid.

Size: 12 inches (30 cm) TL.

Dietary Notes: Omnivorous.

Remarks: A monotypic genus. This rare and often expensive species is only sporadically available. Reproduction is only reported in very old specimens in captivity, and they are known to be poor parents, with egg cannibalism being a common problem.

Hypselecara coryphaenoides
(HECKEL 1840)

Trade Name: Chocolate cichlid.
Size: 10 inches (25 cm) TL.
Dietary Notes: Omnivorous.
Remarks: This is one of those must-have species of rare cichlids. It is best to provide a large aquarium with ample hiding places—driftwood or artificial plants. This is a long-lived species that does very well with other moderately-sized cichlids.

Hypselacara temporalis
(GÜNTHER 1862)

6.6	6.8	7.0

Trade Name: Chocolate cichlid.

Size: 12 inches (30 cm) TL.

Dietary Notes: Omnivorous.

Remarks: An excellent species for the peaceful community aquarium of large cichlids, this fish is normally only aggressive when breeding, and even this aggression is only directed at those fishes that wish to disrupt the nest. This large-growing fish is highly recommended for the hobbyist who likes big fish with a small attitude.

Mesonauta festivus
(HECKEL 1840)

| 6.6 | 6.8 | 7.0 |

21.1 26.6 32.2 37.7 °C
70   80   90   100 °F

Trade Name: Festivum, flag cichlid.

Size: 8 inches (20 cm) TL.

Dietary Notes: Omnivorous.

Remarks: Though never very popular, this fish has had a steady presence in the hobby for a very long time. They are tank bred, but many wild fish are also imported. The several species in this genus have been imported at times as festivums. All are very peaceful cichlids.

Mesonauta insignis
(HECKEL 1840)

  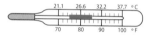

Trade Name: Festivum, flag cichlid.

Size: 8 inches (20 cm) TL.

Dietary Notes: Omnivorous.

Remarks: All of the fish in this genus are very similar in appearance and are identical in care and husbandry.

Pterophyllum altum
PELLEGRIN 1903

| 6.4 | 6.6 | 6.8 |

Trade Name: Altum angel.

Size: 8 inches (20 cm) TH (total height).

Dietary Notes: Omnivorous.

Remarks: Care and husbandry is generally the same as with scalare angels, but they need more attention paid to the quality of their water. Since nearly all of them are still wild collected, it is best to make sure their water is very warm, soft, acid, and has a low bacterial count. This species is not recommended for beginners. It is rarely bred in captivity.

Pterophyllum leopoldi
(GOSSE 1963)

| 6.4 | 6.6 | 6.8 |

Trade Name: One-spot angelfish.

Size: 6 inches (15 cm) TH.

Dietary Notes: Omnivorous.

Remarks: Previously known as *Pterophyllum dumerilii*, these are hardy and robust angels once they have been properly acclimated. Like altum angels, these are almost always wild collected, and this species is also not recommended for beginners. Commercial angel breeders have used this species to put wild blood into their stock.

Pterophyllum scalare
(LICHTENSTEIN 1823)

6.4	6.6	6.8

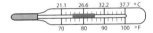

21.1 26.6 32.2 37.7 °C
70   80   90   100 °F

Trade Name: Silver angelfish.

Size: 6 inches (15 cm) TH.

Dietary Notes: Omnivorous.

Remarks: Probably the most recognizable freshwater aquarium fish throughout the world, the angelfish is often not recognized as a cichlid. There are literally dozens of domesticated strains to choose from. Provide a tall aquarium containing soft, warm water of a slightly acidic pH. Frequent water changes are a must with all angelfishes and with good care these beauties will often spawn. Sometimes males battle, so make sure that they're not overcrowded. Usually a pair to 20 gallons (76 l) works well.

Region 6 • South America

Black Lace Veil Angel

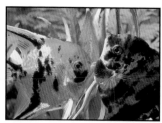

Marble Angel

Black Lace Angel

Half-Black Angel

Blue/Black Angel

Gold Angel

Please see remarks on page 319 regarding care and husbandry.

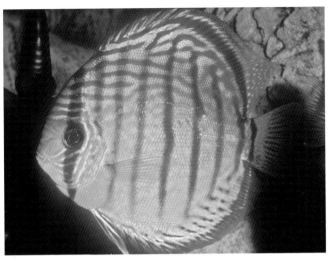

Symphysodon aequifasciatus
PELLEGRIN 1904

6.4	6.6	6.8

Trade Names: Discus, blue discus.

Size: 8 inches (20 cm) TL.

Dietary Notes: Omnivorous.

Remarks: This cichlid has a fandom the world over, with dozens of domesticated varieties. They are best kept alone, in very warm, soft, acid water. Even more than the closely related angelfish, discus benefit highly from frequent, large-scale water changes.

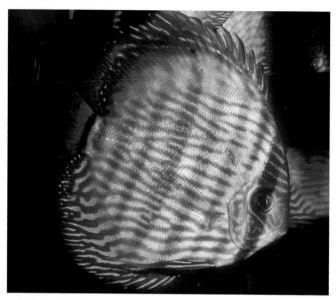

Symphysodon discus
Heckel 1840

| 6.4 | 6.6 | 6.8 |

Trade Names: Discus, Heckel discus.

Size: 8 inches (20 cm) TL.

Dietary Notes: Omnivorous.

Remarks: Unlike the *S. aequifasciatus*, this species is rarely
bred in home aquariums and they do not have nearly the
number of man-made color varieties available either. The
most distinguishing feature of the Heckle Discus is their
broad center bar, which extends from the base of the dorsal
fin down to the ventral region at about the middle of the
body.

Super Red Turquoise Discus

Ocean Green Discus

Marlboro Red Discus

Blue Diamond Discus

Tangerine Discus

Red Panda Discus

Please see remarks on page 322
regarding care and husbandry.

Uaru amphiacanthoides
HECKEL 1840

6.4	6.6	6.8

Trade Names: Uaru (waroo).

Size: 12 inches (30 cm) TL.

Dietary Notes: Mainly herbivorous.

Remarks: Uaru are large, generally peaceful cichlids that relish feedings of plant-based materials and do well with other large cichlids of similar size and temperament. Adults may become quite belligerent if they pair up and look to spawn.

Uaru fernandezyepezi
STAWIKOWSKI 1989

| 6.4 | 6.6 | 6.8 |

Trade Name: Long-finned waroo.
Size: 12 inches (30 cm) TL.
Dietary Notes: Mainly herbivorous.
Remarks: This rather new and exciting cichlid comes from two main river systems; the Rio Atabapo in Colombia and the Rio Orinoco in Venezuela and Colombia. They are generally peaceful but are very sensitive to dissolved metabolites in their water. Be sure to have good filtration and perform frequent water changes.

Geophaginae

This subfamily contains three tribes. The dwarf cichlids of South America are found in two of the tribes: Crenicaratini and Geophagini.

Acarichthyini

The fish in the two genera in this tribe are similar to the eartheaters Geophagini. Many consider them intermediate between *Geophagus* and *Aequidens*.

Acarichthys heckelii
(MÜLLER & TROSCHEL 1849)

6.8	7.0	7.2

Trade Names: Threadfin acara, threadfin cichlid.

Size: 6 inches (15 cm) TL.

Dietary Notes: A sandsifter.

Remarks: The long extensions on the dorsal fin give it the common name "threadfin." This is a substrate spawner, which often lays the eggs on the roof of a cave.

Guianacara geayi
(PELLEGRIN 1902)

6.8	7.0	7.2

Size: 3 inches (9 cm) TL.

Dietary Notes: A sand-sifter.

Remarks: There are several species in this genus. All are peaceful, gregarious cichlids that live in colonies, but at spawning the pairs can be very aggressive.

327

CRENICARATINI

These are the checkerboard cichlids and their kin. Unlike the dwarf Geophagini species, this tribe of dwarf cichlids is not well known or well represented in the hobby, but it should be. Ranging from tiny to medium in size, they are big in potential appeal as aquarium specimens.

Natural History & Aquarium Husbandry

Not surprisingly, not a lot is known about these species. They come from blackwater habitats for the most part, and many have demonstrated spawning difficulties in hard water, especially with poor hatch rates. Very soft, warm, acid water seems to be the key to success. Many, if not all, species are harem spawners.

They appear to be micropredators, though they certainly will consume algae and probably detritus in the leaf litter many of them inhabit. Captive specimens relish small live foods, and wild-caught fish may refuse prepared foods.

As with other South American dwarfs, dither fish are extremely important, but in contrast to apistos, having other fish in the tank has been found by several aquarists to be necessary for spawning success with many of these cichlids.

Dicrossus filamentosus is a very handsome species that does well in aquariums.

Crenicara punctulatum
(GÜNTHER 1863)

  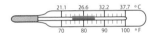

Trade Name: Checkerboard cichlid.

Size: 4 inches (10 cm) TL.

Dietary Notes: A micropredator.

Remarks: This widespread Amazonian species is a protogynous hermaphrodite—the first confirmed hermaphrody in cichlids. Juveniles are female, and at maturity one in each group becomes the harem's male.

Dicrossus filamentosus
(LADIGES 1958)

6.8	7.0	7.2

Trade Name: Lyretail checkerboard cichlid.

Size: 1.5 inches (4 cm) TL.

Dietary Notes: A micropredator.

Remarks: This is probably the best known of the checkerboard cichlids, and it isn't that common in the hobby. The male develops the eponymous lyretail.

Dicrossus maculatus
STEINDACHNER 1875

  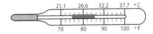

Trade Name: Checkerboard cichlid.

Size: 2 inches (5.5 cm) TL.

Dietary Notes: A micropredator.

Remarks: This cichlid is quite rare in the hobby, though some people are breeding them. Juveniles and females are hard to distinguish from *D. filamentosus*.

GEOPHAGINI

Two major groups of cichlids with a great many species are found in this tribe: the eartheaters and a second set of South American dwarfs, and both have dedicated followings in the hobby. One species is found in North America and will be covered in the next chapter.

The eartheaters show enormous diversity in reproductive strategies (substrate spawners and ovophilous and larvophilous mouthbrooders), and they gained popularity many years ago as the only mouthbrooding neotropical cichlids. Since that time mouthbrooding, at least facultative mouthbrooding, has been found among other geophagines and the heroines.

The dwarfs comprise four genera: *Apistogramma*, *Apistogrammoides*, *Mikrogeophagus*, and *Taeniacara*. These tiny cichlids are extremely widespread, extremely diverse, and extremely popular, both among cichlid fanciers and among aquarists with a preference for small-tank fishes like killies and anabantoids.

The dwarf species and many of the large ones are quite peaceful, but one must not be complacent. Some species are much more aggressive than others. Most geophagophiles consider *Geophagus brasiliensis* to be one of the aggressive species, but your experience may differ.

Natural History & Captive Husbandry

While the dwarfs share a lot of features with the larger eartheaters, they tend to live among the leaf litter of small, shallow streams rather than to sift the sand of larger and deeper habitats. Smaller aquaria with a layer of waterlogged dried leaves on the bottom and a couple of pieces of wood or rock for a hiding and spawning cave are perfect for *Apistogramma*. They are likely to make themselves scarce unless the tank includes some dither fish—a school of small tetras serves very well. Apistos are cryptic spawners, though some prefer hiding places near the surface as opposed to on the bottom. The very similar *Mikrogeophagus*, however, typically spawns in the open, usually on a flat rock.

The larger species do best when supplied with a substrate of fine sand in which they can indulge their natural inclination to sift sand through their gill rakers in search of edible tidbits. As general detritivores and micropredators, these fishes do well on any balanced prepared diet.

The dwarf geophagines are almost all from warm, very soft, acid streams, and many require that type of water for successful spawning. The larger species come from a bit more diversity of habitat. As usual, knowing where your fish come from is a great help in deciding what conditions to provide.

Apistos

Many species show a variety of breeding behaviors, including some elaborate excavation and fortressing of the nest site. Aquarists often note a difference between the behaviors of wild-caught and tank-raised specimens. Some aquarists have reported apparent sex changes in adult apistos, especially *A. nijsenni*.

Apistos show marked dimorphism. The males are larger, with more elaborate finnage and colors. In many species, the female turns yellow at spawning time. The female cares for the eggs and fry, while the male defends the territory.

Although many specialists breed their apistos in pairs in small—5- or 10-gallon (20- to 40-l)—tanks, a fuller range of behaviors, including harem spawning, sneaker males, etc., can only be observed if they are maintained in a well-planted larger tanks say, a 6-foot (180-cm) aquarium.

The species from extreme blackwater conditions may not spawn if the water is not sufficiently soft and acid, or the eggs will not be viable. Many aquarists use rain water or RO, combined with peat and dried leaves, to provide water extremely low in pH and in conductivity.

With so many species, it may be hard for an aquarist to decide where to start. If in doubt, go with one of the ABC apistos: *A. agassizii*, *A. borelli*, and *A. cacatuoides*. The long-term popularity of these three apistos attests to their adaptability and general appeal.

Captive specimens sometimes grow larger than wild fish. While not as extreme as is seen among Malawi mbuna, this phenomenon can add an inch (2.5 cm) to the listed sizes of these species.

Eartheaters

Cichlids in the genera *Biotodoma*, *Geophagus*, *Gymnogeophagus*, and *Satanoperca* are generally regarded as eartheaters. The demonfish, genus *Satanoperca*, are so named because of native tribes' beliefs.

Adapted to obtain their food by sifting detritus and small invertebrates out of the substrate, these fish are among the most colorful of South American cichlids. A variety of breeding strategies are employed by these fishes, including immediate and delayed mouthbrooding.

They all require large tanks and very clean water. The northernmost species prefer medium to hard water, neutral to slightly basic. Most of the Amazonian species prefer, if not demand soft, acid water. The southernmost species (*Gymnogeophagus*) are subtropical and prefer cooler temperatures and harder, neutral to slightly basic water. In fact, they generally require a "winter" of cooler temperatures, down to 60°F (15°C).

Long a taxonomic confusion, this group has undergone extensive revision, but much remains to be done. We include a group of to-be-reassigned species, listed as "*Geophagus*."

Apistogramma agassizii
(Steindachner 1875)

Size: 3 inches (7.5 cm) TL.

Dietary Notes: A micropredator.

Remarks: This widespread species is probably the best known apisto. It comes in several color forms and geographical variants. Like many in this genus, it is a harem spawner. To many exporters, this is the default species (see *A*. cf. *agassizii*).

Apistogramma bitaeniata
Pellegrin 1936
Size: 2 inches (5 cm) TL.

Apistogramma borellii
(Regan 1906)
Size: 2 inches (5 cm) TL.

Apistogramma cacatuoides
Hoedeman 1951
Size: 2 inches (5 cm) TL;
females smaller.

Apistogramma cf. agassizii
Undescribed to Date
Size: 3 inches (7.5 cm) TL.

Apistogramma diplotaenia
Kullander 1987
Size: 2 inches (5 cm) TL.

Apistogramma elizabethae
Kullander 1980
Size: 3 inches (7.5 cm) TL.

Please see remarks opposite
regarding care and husbandry.

Apistogramma eunotus
KULLANDER 1981

| 6.8 | 7.0 | 7.2 |

Size: 2 inches (5 cm) TL.

Dietary Notes: A micropredator.

Remarks: This is a species with a restricted range, but still it seems to exhibit some variation in color. It is one of the higher-priced apistos. All *Apistogramma* have the same basic care and husbandry requirements in aquariums. Since they're dwarf cichlids, and usually attain sizes of around 3 inches (9 cm) TL, they can easily be kept in small aquariums as long as they are not overcrowded. Additionally, they can be kept in community aquariums with other peaceful fishes.

337

Apistogramma gibbeceps
Meinken 1969
Size: 2 inches (5 cm) TL.

Apistogramma juruensis
Kullander 1986
Size: 3 inches (7.5 cm) TL.

Apistogramma macmasteri
Kullander 1979
Size: 2.75 inches (7 cm) TL;
females smaller.

Apistogramma mendezi
Römer 1994
Size: 4 inches (10 cm) TL;
usually smaller.

Apistogramma nijsseni
Kullander 1979
Size: 2 inches (5 cm) TL.

Apistogramma norberti
Staeck 1991
Size: 2 inches (5 cm) TL.

Please see remarks on page 337
regarding care and husbandry.

Apistogramma panduroil
Römen 1997
Size: 3 inches (7.5 cm) TL.

Apistogramma pertensis
Haseman 1991
Size: 2 inches (5 cm) TL.

Apistogramma trifasciata
(Eigenmann & Kennedy 1903)
Size: 2 inches (5 cm) TL.

Apistogramma uaupesi
Kullander 1980
Size: 2.75 inches (7 cm) TL.

Apistogramma viejita
Kullander 1979
Size: 2 inches (5 cm) TL.

Apistogramma eunotus
Kullander 1981
Size: 3 inches (7.5 cm) TL.

Please see remarks on page 337
regarding care and husbandry.

339

Biotodoma cupido
(HECKEL 1840)

Size: 4 inches (10 cm) TL.

Dietary Notes: A sand-sifter.

Remarks: This peaceful small cichlid and its congener *B. wavrini* are only occasionally available, as there appears to be small demand for them. They are very peaceful cichlids.

Geophagus altifrons
Heckel 1840
Size: 10 inches (25 cm) TL.

Geophagus proximus
(Castelnau 1855)
Size: 8 inches (20 cm) TL.

"Geophagus" brasiliensis
(Quoy & Gaimard 1824)
Size: 11 inches (28 cm) TL.

***"Geophagus* sp." red head Tapajos"**
Undescribed to Date
Size: 8 inches (20 cm) TL.

***"Geophagus"* sp. "altamiara"**
Undescribed to Date
Size: 8 inches (20 cm) TL.

***"Geophagus"* sp. "red bahia"**
Undescribed to Date
Size: 8 inches (20 cm) TL.

Please see remarks on page 342
regarding care and husbandry.

Geophagus surinamensis
(Bloch 1791)

6.8	7.0	7.2

Size: 8 inches (20 cm) TL.

Dietary Notes: A sand-sifter.

Remarks: Yet another species (there may be more than one) that is hardly ever correctly identified in the trade. The red and neon blue stripes are distinctive. This is a larvophilous biparental mouthbrooder. The parents care for the fry for a long time. Substrates for aquariums containing *Geophagus* species should be sandy or at least of a fine particle size. This will ensure that the substrate doesn't get caught in their buccal cavities while they are sifting through it…after all, *Geophagus* means eartheating!

"Geophagus" steindachneri
EIGENMANN & HILDEBRAND 1910

6.8	7.0	7.2

Trade Name: Redhump eartheater.

Size: 10 inches (25 cm) TL.

Dietary Notes: A sand-sifter.

Remarks: This is one of the most popular species of eartheaters. They are easily recognized by their red hump (in males) and red patch of color in the nuchal region (in females). Sometimes their lips are red as well. Their care in aquariums is simple, and since so many are produced commercially now, there is little need to provide special water conditions for them.

Gymnogeophagus australis
(Eigenmann 1907)
Size: 6 inches (15 cm) TL.

Gymnogeophagus balzanii
(Perugia 1891
Size: 7 inches (18 cm) TL.

Gymnogeophagus labiatus
(Hensel 1870)
Size: 8 inches (20 cm) TL.

Gymnogeophagus meridionalis
Reis & Malabarba 1988
Size: 4.75 inches (12 cm) TL.

Gymnogeophagus rhabdotus
(Hensel 1870)
Size: 6 inches (15 cm) TL.

Gymnogeophagus sp. "rio salto"
Undescribed to Date
Size: 8 inches (20 cm) TL.

Please see remarks opposite
regarding care and husbandry.

Gymnogeophagus gymnogenys
(HENSEL 1870)

| 6.6 | 6.8 | 7.0 |

Size: 8 inches (20 cm) TL.

Dietary Notes: A sand-sifter.

Remarks: Some specimens of *G. gymnogenys* are gorgeous, with their bright red fins and nearly metallic yellow and lime green nuchal region and flanks. Many hobbyists have been exploring different tankmates that are suitable with this and other subtropical *Gymnogeophagus* species and are finding that many fishes that are native to the United States make good tankmates for them.

Mikrogeophagus altispinosa
(HASEMAN 1911)

6.6	6.8	7.0

Trade Names: Bolivian ram, butterfly ram.

Size: 3 inches (7.5 cm) TL.

Dietary Notes: Feeds on small invertebrates and detritus.

Remarks: The two miniature eartheaters in this genus are beautiful and popular, but in order to succeed with them, you must provide soft, acid water that is very warm—80°F (27°C) or higher. They will typically spawn in the open, or a flat horizontal surface.

Mikrogeophagus ramirezi
(MYERS & HARRY 1948)

6.6	6.8	7.0

Size: 2.5 inches (6 cm) TL.

Dietary Notes: Feeds on small invertebrates and detritus.

Remarks: Perhaps the most popular dwarf cichlid next to *Apistogramma cacatuoides*, *M. ramirezi* is colorful and peaceful. Because of this and its similar water requirements, it is often kept with discus. Several domesticated morphs have been developed, including long finned and xanthic.

Satanoperca acuticeps
(Heckel 1840)
Size: 8 inches (20 cm) TL.

Satanoperca daemon
(Heckel 1840)
Size: 10 inches (25 cm) TL.

Satanoperca daemon
(Heckel 1840)
Size: 10 inches (25 cm) TL.

Satanoperca jurupari
(Heckel 1840)
Size: 10 inches (25 cm) TL.

Satanoperca jurupari
(Heckel 1840)
Size: 10 inches (25 cm) TL.

Satanoperca lilith
Kullander & Ferreira 1988
Size: 10 inches (25 cm) TL.

Please see remarks opposite
regarding care and husbandry.

Satanoperca leucosticta
(MÜLLER & TROSCHEL 1848)

6.6	6.8	7.0

Size: 8 inches (20 cm) TL.

Dietary Notes: A sand-sifter.

Remarks: This species was for a long time confused with *S. jurupari*. There remain several distinct populations of this cichlid that may be one day be broken into one or more new species. Some are larvophilous mouthbrooders, while others are ovophilous. Members of *Satanoperca* require warm, soft water with a slightly acidic pH. Just as with *Geophagus*, *Satanoperca* need a sand substrate so the particles don't get caught in their mouths.

Taeniacara candidi
MYERS 1935

| 6.6 | 6.8 | 7.0 |

Size: 2.75 inches (7 cm) TL.

Dietary Notes:

Remarks: Monotypic genus. This is a blackwater dwarf similar to the apistos. It has proven difficult to spawn, perhaps because of strict water chemistry requirements. It is peaceful and can be kept in a community setting.

Chapter 9

Region 7
North America

HEROINI, AGAIN

Cichlidae's presence in North America is restricted to Central America, Mexico, and a bit of the southeastern United States. Temperature seems to have been a limiting factor in their northward spread. Many cichlids have become firmly established in subtropical Florida, where their northward distribution is bounded by minimum temperatures. It is thought that the presence of Centrarchidae, the sunfish, which occupy much the same niches as Cichlidae, stood in the way of the development of coolwater cichlids in North America; i.e., not having readily available niches, cichlids would gain no advantage from developing cold tolerance. Note that in South America, where there are no native centrarchids, southernmost cichlid species occur in subtropical, indeed almost temperate, habitats.

Although the tribe Heroni has a respectable showing in South America, it truly shines in North America, where, with the exception of a close relative in the tribe Cichlasomatini and one in Geophagini that barely make it out of South America, it represents all of the cichlids on the continent. So, let's get the exceptions out of the way, then move on to the Central American heroines.

A LEFTOVER CICHLASOMATINE

When new land masses rise out of the sea, freshwater fishes can use the interconnectedness of streams and rivers to colonize the new aquatic habitats, so it is not surprising that the northernmost South American cichlids have a modern presence in Panama and Costa Rica. The one cichlasomatine outside South America is one of the species orphaned by the revision of *Aequidens*, a member of the green terror-blue acara complex.

"Aequidens" coeruleopuntcatus
(KNER & STEINDACHNER 1863)

Size: 6 inches (15 cm) TL.

Dietary Notes: An omnivore.

Remarks: A robust and moderately aggressive cichlid. Their color is an emerald green, and males have a distinct forehead and long-flowing fins.

THE REST ARE HEROINES

Although many cichlids retain the primitive characteristic of tolerance for salinity, the heroines of North America often display even a preference for brackish conditions. This was undoubtedly instrumental in their colonization of the new niches opened up when the Panamanian Isthmus appeared a few million years ago. By swimming along the seashore from river mouth to river mouth they were able to make their way northward without requiring full-freshwater connections between various river drainages. They eventually colonized Mesoamerican rivers and volcanic lakes and finally reached what is now the Southwest United States.

It is not believed, however, that marine migration accounts for the presence of cichlids on some Caribbean islands. It is one thing to move along coastal estuaries and quite another to take off through an open stretch of ocean. As we discussed in Chapter 1, it is unlikely that cichlids can traverse open sea successfully (even though some species definitely make regular forays into inshore reef areas. Direct trans-marine migration is also unlikely when we consider that some islands much closer to the mainland do not have cichlid populations while ones further out do.

The mechanism or mechanisms by which certain islands were colonized by cichlids are uncertain. Certainly their salt tolerance might enable them to survive a freak mega hurricane or tsunami washing them from the mainland onto an island. Other suggestions include cichlid eggs or larvae being stuck on a wading bird's feet or feathers. Human intervention is even a remote possibility.

TAXONOMIC ISSUES

From a taxonomic point of view, North American cichlids sometimes seem like Malawi mbuna—jumping from genus to genus as biologists try to sort out all the interrelationships. Subgenera are elevated to generic status, species are assigned and reassigned, and considerable confusion obtains.

The following classifications are perhaps a bit subjective and eclectic, following one system in one place and a different system in another place, but it is close to what most aquarists specializing in this group of cichlids are familiar with. Once again, we sacrifice a desire for complete accuracy to the goal of hobbyist utility.

Even so, you may occasionally find several of the following species listed under a different genus from where they are here. As just one example, you may find *Cryptoheros panamensis* listed elsewhere as *Neetroplus panamensis*. So, if you cannot find a certain species, be sure to check in other genera.

A note on *Cichlasoma*: since it is now recognized that none of the North American cichlids are *Cichlasoma*, some people stick all of the species into one genus or another, just to get them out of *Cichlasoma*. Here we follow those who maintain a "slush pile" of orphaned and unassigned species (as we did for *Aequidens* and *Cichlasoma* in South America), which we call "*Cichlasoma*."

While we used the example of separating *Amphilophus* and *Vieja* at opposite ends of the book as something we wanted to avoid in this reference, we are faced with the decision of what to do here, and whether they should wind up at opposite ends of the chapter. Once again we have deferred to pragmatic utility and decided to list these fish alphabetically by genera. All the species in this chapter are closely related, and, as I mentioned, several have been moved from genus to genus, some several times.

If we try to maintain a fiction that the number of pages between two cichlids in this chapter has a direct relationship to their relatedness, that fact alone would reveal the man behind the curtain. Having narrowed down your search to the North American heroines, you may have to flip a few pages to compare the most closely related species in some instances.

On the other hand, the adaptive radiation of this tribe has produced a wide variety of types, which are reflected in the different genera. Thus, we will give a few notes about each genus prior to listing representative species. Among these notes will be some comments about the apparent affinity between genera.

This means, however, that there is no way to split this cumbersome final chapter on logical or biological grounds. Simply to arbitrarily divide the genera at some letter of the alphabet in order to make shorter chapters is insufficient motivation, and it is fitting that we end this world tour of cichlids with a mega chapter, since it describes a massive continental invasion by a single group of cichlids that radiated

Parachromis dovii is still commonly referred to *"Cichlasoma" dovii*.

into a plethora of forms, whose taxonomy is far from complete. Such is the story of Cichlidae, told over and over on four continents.

Natural History & Captive Husbandry

North America's cichlids come for the most part from volcanic lakes and mountain streams. The general lack of extensive floodplains in this narrow piece of continent precludes habitats like blackwater streams; instead most habitats contain moderately hard to hard water with neutral to basic pH. These fish are usually quite adaptable, but the use of soluble substrates and rocks will help guard against pH drop.

Actually, these heavy feeding fishes will greatly benefit from a water-change regimen that doesn't give the water time to drop in pH from metabolic wastes. Many of them are particularly sensitive to dissolved metabolites, and HLLE is a common consequence of laxness with the water changes. Large tanks, heavy filtration, and copious water changes will do more to keep these hardy, long-lived cichlids hearty and living long than anything else.

Many species, especially the smaller ones, can be maintained in cichlid communities with like-minded fishes. The larger or more aggressive species, however, often must be kept not only in single-species tanks but even in single-fish tanks. It is safest to maintain breeding pairs with a partial divider, either one that permits the smaller female passage but not the male, or one that enables them to spawn on the bottom at the divider without ever coming into contact with each other.

Although many treat these cichlids as meat eaters, they are almost all true omnivores, and plants—including seeds and fruit—make up a good portion of their diets. Of course, even specialized piscivores eat a lot of vegetable matter, at least in the guts of their prey. In captivity they do best when fed an omnivorous diet, with chunks of meat and live invertebrates as treats. Favorites include crickets, mealworms, earthworms, snails, crayfish, and feeder roaches, all of which should be gut loaded before use—a quality flake food is perfect for this.

AMPHILOPHUS

This genus contains many medium to moderately large species, ranging from mildly to very aggressive. They tend to be late maturing, with large spawns that are ferociously defended.

Natural polymorphism occurs in the Midas-complex (*A. citrinellus*, *A. labiatus*, and others), and there is evidence of assortative pairing in the wild. In addition, there appears to be niche specialization, specifically with the xanthic forms preferring deepwater habitats.

Evolutionary biologists are especially interested in this group of fishes because of its apparent speciation and incipient speciation, including perhaps sympatric speciation. Some authors extrapolate from these findings to Malawian BB-O-OB polymorphy.

Amphilophus zaliosus, **the arrow cichlid.**

Amphilophus alfari
(Meek 1907)
Size: 6 inches (15 cm) TL.

Amphilophus altifrons
(Kner 1863)
Size: 6 inches (15 cm) TL.

Amphilophus amarillo
Stauffer & McKaye 2002
Size: 6 inches (15 cm) TL, maybe
slightly larger.

Amphilophus calobrensis
(Meek & Hildebrand 1913)
Size: 10 inches (25 cm) TL.

Amphilophus diquis
(Bussing 1974)
Size: 6 inches (15 cm) TL.

Amphilophus citrinellus
(Günther 1864)
Size: 12 inches (30 cm) TL.

Please see remarks on page 358
regarding care and husbandry.

Amphilophus citrinellus
(GÜNTHER 1864)

| 7.0 | 7.2 | 7.4 |

21.1 26.6 32.2 37.7 °C
70 80 90 100 °F

Trade Names: Midas cichlid, red devil.

Size: 12 inches (30 cm) TL.

Dietary Notes: Omnivorous.

Remarks: This aggressive cichlid comes from the Atlantic slope of Nicaragua and Costa Rica, especially in Lakes Nicaragua, Managua, Masaya, and Apoyo. It is often confused with *A. labiatus*, and unfortunately, many specimens in the hobby today are hybrids.

Amphilophus citrinellus
(Günther 1864)
Size: 12 inches (30 cm) TL.

Amphilophus hogaboomorum
(Carr & Giovannoli 1950)
Size: 6 inches (15 cm) TL.

Amphilophus longimanus
(Günther 1867)
Size: 6 inches (15 cm) TL.

Amphilophus lyonsi
(Gosse 1966)
Size: 8 inches (20 cm) TL.

Amphilophus macracanthus
(Günther 1864)
Size: 10 inches (25 cm) TL.

Amphilophus nourissati
(Allgayer 1989)
Size: 10 inches (25 cm) TL.

Please see remarks on page 358
regarding care and husbandry.

Amphilophus labiatus
(GÜNTHER 1864)

Trade Names: Red devil, Midas cichlid.
Size: 10 inches (25 cm) TL.
Dietary Notes: Omnivorous.
Remarks: Often confused with *A. citrinellus*, this perennial favorite hails from the Atlantic slope of Nicaragua in Lakes Nicaragua and Managua. It is difficult to make sure aquarium-raised individuals are genetically pure.

Amphilophus rhytisma
(López 1983)
Size: 6 inches (15 cm) TL.

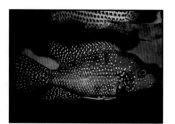

Amphilophus rostratus
(Gill 1877)
Size: 8 inches (20 cm) TL.

Amphilophus sagittae
Stauffer & McKaye 2002
Size: 8 inches (20 cm) TL.

Amphilophus xiloaensis
Stauffer & McKaye 2002
Size: 6 inches (15 cm) TL.

Amphilophus zaliosus
(Barlow 1976)
Size: 8 inches (20 cm) TL.

Amphilophus trimaculatus
See page 366 for details!

Please see remarks on page 358
regarding care and husbandry.

Amphilophus robertsoni
(REGAN 1905)

| 7.0 | 7.2 | 7.4 |

Size: 8 inches (20 cm) TL.

Dietary Notes: Feeds primarily by sifting substrate for detritus and invertebrates.

Remarks: From the Atlantic slope of Mexico to Honduras, this species is a candidate for the cichlid with the most beautiful blue spangling. It does not get along well with conspecifics, unless you have a compatible pair.

Amphilophus trimaculatus
(GÜNTHER 1867)

7.0	7.2	7.4

Trade Names: Trimac, three-spot cichlid.

Size: 16 inches (40 cm) TL.

Dietary Notes: Primarily a predator.

Remarks: From the Pacific slope, Mexico to El Salvador, this fish is found in habitats ranging from acidic swamps to marine river deltas. This is a big cichlid with a big chip on its shoulder. It is used as a base for the hybrid flowerhorns, and it's getting tough to find pure-blood specimens. Some list this species in *Amphilophus*.

Uncertain South American ex-*Cichlasoma*

There are a few South American species that surprise many people in that they resemble North American cichlids and are often thought of as Central American fishes, though they are not. Some consider them *Amphilophus*. Calling them "*Cichlasoma*" confuses them with the already complicated leftover South American *Cichlasoma* orphans, but these are heroines. So, we've stuck the Central American-like South Americans here, as their care is the same. If they are eventually confirmed in *Amphilophus*, these South Americans will be the southernmost representatives of a primarily North American genus.

Adult male Ex-*Cichlasoma festae*.

Ex-*Cichlasoma atromaculatum*
REGAN 1912

Trade Name: "*Amphilophus atromaculatus.*"

Size: 10 inches (25 cm) TL.

Dietary Notes: An omnivore.

Remarks: Found in Colombia, this cichlid exhibits sexual dichromatism, with female breeding coloration than can include a red belly and iridescent blue on the dorsal fin, much like many Central American species.

Ex-*Cichlasoma festae*
(BOULENGER 1899)

Trade Names: "*Amphilophus festae*," festae, red terror.

Size: 20 inches (50 cm) TL.

Dietary Notes: Eats primarily benthic invertebrates.

Remarks: From Pacific drainages of Ecuador to Peru, this orange to red monster is a favorite tank buster. It is reported established in Florida, where it is often called an "oscar," a generic term for any big cichlid.

Archocentrus

The convict cichlids were recently removed from this genus, shortly after being established in it, leaving it monotypic in some people's view, since they feel *A. octofasciatus* and *A. spinosissimus* are different enough to belong in other genera. For now they remain within *Archocentrus*.

Archocentrus centrarchus
(GILL & BRANSFORD 1877)

7.0	7.2	7.4

Trade Name: Flier cichlid.**Size:** 5 inches (12.5 cm) TL.

Dietary Notes: An omnivore.

Remarks: This species from Honduras and Costa Rica is not as popular as it should be. These small but interesting cichlids are quite comical and prolific in home aquariums. They like to hang the newly hatched fry on vertical surfaces, and the fry feed in part off their parents' body slime.

Archocentrus octofasciatus
(REGAN 1903)

| 7.0 | 7.2 | 7.4 |

Trade Name: Jack Dempsey.

Size: 10 inches (25 cm) TL.

Dietary Notes: An omnivore.

Remarks: Found from Mexico to Belize, the Jack Dempsey was named for the famous boxer back when this was about the nastiest cichlid in the hobby. Today it is considered mildly aggressive. Adult males are breathtaking with their blue spangles and sometimes a red top edge to the dorsal. A couple of domesticated strains have been developed, including the unusual blue morph.

Archocentrus spinosissimus
(VAILLANT & PELLEGRIN 1902)

Size: 6 inches (15 cm) TL.

Dietary Notes: An omnivore.

Remarks: This Guatemalan cichlid is one of those heroines that is sprinkled with black dots over the whole body and the fins. In addition, it has beautiful iridescences.

Chuco

In the taxonomic confusion that is North American Cichlidae, one of the foci is the genus *Vieja*, which most consider to be multiply polyphyletic. At the moment, one of the solutions includes subdividing that mega-genus, and one of the subdivisions is the genus *Chuco*, which winds up with three species, and probably several more that remain undescribed.

Chuco godmanni
(GÜNTHER 1862)

  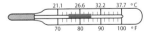

Trade Name: Southern checkmark cichlid.
Size: 12 inches (30 cm) TL.
Dietary Notes: An omnivore, feeds on a lot of vegetation.
Remarks: Found in fast-flowing mountain rivers of the Polochic River drainage on the Atlantic slope. Individuals of all ages often show a bold black mark that resembles a checkmark. This is very apparent on wild-collected individuals.

Chuco intermedius
(GÜNTHER 1862)

7.0	7.2	7.4

Trade Name: Northern checkmark cichlid.

Size: 8 inches (20 cm) TL.

Dietary Notes: An omnivore.

Remarks: Found on the Atlantic slope of Mexico, Guatemala, and Belize, this cichlid is identifiable by a black mark that closely resembles an "L" on its side. This mark, similar to *C. godmanni*'s, is present throughout their lives at all stages, and it is more apparent in wild-collected individuals, just as in *C. godmanni*.

Chuco microphthalmus
(GÜNTHER 1862)

Size: 10 inches (25 cm) TL.

Dietary Notes: An omnivore.

Remarks: From the Atlantic slope of Guatemala and Honduras, this cichlid is less aggressive than its two congeners. Their metallic gold speckles make them very visible in the aquarium under proper illumination, even at a distance.

"Cichlasoma"

As mentioned, these ex-*Cichlasoma* species are placed by many into a variety of other genera, just to get them out of *Cichlasoma*, since no North American cichlids are in that genus. There is little agreement, however, on where each should be, and it is still possible some may be placed in new genera. Since we are using genera like *Amphilophus*, *Nandopsis*, and *Herichthys sensu stricto*, we use this slush-pile genus for these yet-to-be-assigned species.

Adult male *"Cichlasoma" grammodes*.

"Cichlasoma" beani
(JORDAN 1888)

| 7.0 | 7.2 | 7.4 |

Size: 12 inches (30 cm) TL.

Dietary Notes: An omnivore.

Remarks: Found on the Pacific slope of Mexico, this is a big, aggressive cichlid. They are not outrageously colorful, but their pleasing pattern of eight to nine blotches arranged along their flanks makes them intriguing and different.

"Cichlasoma" grammodes
Taylor & Miller 1980
Size: 12 inches (30 cm) TL.

"Cichlasoma" heterospilum
(Hubbs 1936)
Size: 10 inches (25 cm) TL.

"Cichlasoma" istlanum
(Jordan & Snyder, 1899)
Size: 12 inches (30 cm) TL.

"Cichlasoma" salvini
(Günther 1862)
Size: 6 inches (15 cm) TL

"Cichlasoma" tuyrense
Meek & Hildebrand 1913
Size: 10 inches (25 cm) TL.

"Cichlasoma" urophthalmus
(Günther 1862)
Size: 10 inches (25 cm) TL.

Please see remarks opposite
for additional information.

"Cichlasoma" bocourti
(VAILLANT & PELLEGRIN 1902)

Size: 12 inches (30 cm) TL.

Dietary Notes: An omnivore.

Remarks: From the Atlantic slope of Guatemala and Belize, this cichlid is left in this slush-pile genus not so much because people haven't gotten around to it as because they aren't sure where to put it. Members of the group *"Cichlasoma"* have the same basic care requirements. A moderately sized or large aquarium that is kept warm and contains plenty of visual barriers would prove to be the best type of setup for these brutes.

"Cichlasoma" pearsei
HUBBS 1936

Size: 8 inches (20 cm) TL.

Dietary Notes: Feeds primarily on aquatic and terrestrial vegetation.

Remarks: Found in freshwater and brackish habitats on the Atlantic slope of southern Mexico into northern Guatemala. Not common in the hobby, this is a beautiful and fairly peaceful large cichlid.

Cryptoheros

The cichlids in this genus, in the convict complex, were recently moved out of *Archocentrus*. Several new species have been discovered in the last decade. All *Cryptoheros* are fine aquarium specimens, and while not usually considered dwarfs because of their feistiness, they are basically miniatures of their larger cousins. They are found from Guatemala to Panama, with some, like *C. nigrofasciatus*, being found practically throughout this range.

Males are typically quite a bit larger than females. Female ornamentation is common, especially red or gold iridescence on the belly, and dorsal fin pigmentation as well. They are cave spawners, and typically extremely easy to breed. They often excavate a crevice under a rock, laying their eggs on the ceiling of the resultant cave. They make excellent parents and frequently raise fry successfully in a community setting. The tankmates, however, may be in danger, as these are spunky little fish, with a much bigger attitude than their body size.

This pair of *Cryptohences sajica* is guarding their fry.

Cryptoheros myrnae
(Loiselle 1997)
Size: 3 inches (8 cm) TL.

Cryptoheros nanoluteus
(Allgayer 1994)
Size: 3 inches (8 cm) TL.

Cryptoheros panamensis
(Meek & Hildebrand 1913)
Size: 6 inches (15 cm) TL.

Cryptoheros septemfasciatus
(Regan 1908)
Size: 4 inches (10 cm) TL.

***Cryptoheros* sp.**
"Honduran redpoint"
Size: 4 inches (10 cm) TL.

***Cryptoheros nigrofasciatus* "OB"**
(Günther 1867)
Size: 4 inches (10 cm) TL.

Please see remarks opposite
regarding care and husbandry.

Cryptoheros nigrofasciatus
(GÜNTHER 1867)

7.0	7.2	7.4

Size: 4 inches (10 cm) TL.

Dietary Notes: An omnivore.

Remarks: Found on both slopes of Guatemala, Honduras, Costa Rica, and Panama, this is the quintessential cichlid. Colorful, spunky, ferocious parents, they top it off with being small enough that you can spawn a pair in a 15- or 20-gallon (50 to 75-liter) tank. To spawn them, just add water! Ironically, not all members of *Cryptoheros* are so easy to spawn, although most are. Often, some tweaking of the water's chemistry will be needed to get them to breed but their basic care is very simple across the board. Warm water, moderate hardness and a neutral to slightly alkaline pH is about it.

Cryptoheros sajica
(Bussing 1974)

| 7.0 | 7.2 | 7.4 |

Trade Name: Blue eyed cichlid, T-bar cichlid.

Size: 3.5 inches (9 cm) TL.

Dietary Notes: An omnivore.

Remarks: Only the older males of this species possess a nuchal hump. They are quite distinctive, with their bluish fins and a broad dark-colored center transverse bar. Both parents become very dark when breeding. Fry may feed off parental mucus.

Cryptoheros spilurus
(GÜNTHER 1862)

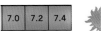 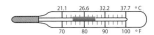

Trade Names: Blue eyed cichlid, *Cryptoheros* "cutteri."

Size: 4.75 inches (12 cm) TL.

Dietary Notes: An omnivore.

Remarks: This cichlid from the Atlantic slope of Belize to Nicaragua has been popular for a long time. It is difficult, however to get pure stock unless you get wild imports, as many convict cichlids have been hybridized in captivity. Current thinking is that *cutteri* is a population of this species.

Herichthys

These are the northernmost cichlids, with the genus ranging from Texas through Mexico to Guatemala. They are large, robust fishes, and they often have breeding coloration that is very different from their normal appearance. In fact, looking at the genus as a whole, their breeding colorations cover all the possible combinations of half-black-half-white patterns.

There is an omnivorous detritivore, a bottom-grubbing molluscivore, and a streamlined piscivore. The three morphs interbreed freely but do not produce hybrids—the young are of whatever morph(s) the parents are. DNA analysis supports that they are the same species.

The molluscivore and the piscivore darken to camouflage themselves when hunting. When spawning, a male of any morph is black, while a female of any morph is white. Truly a fascinating cichlid!

Newly collected *Herichhys labridens*.

Herichthys carpintis
(JORDAN & SNYDER 1899)

Trade Names: Texas cichlid, green Texas cichlid

Size: 8 inches (20 cm) TL.

Dietary Notes: An omnivore.

Remarks: Because this cichlid from the Atlantic slope of Mexico is considerably smaller than *H. cyanoguttatus* but otherwise similar, aquarists think of it as a junior version, perfect for less-large tanks. This is comparable to the pairing in hobbyists' minds of "*C.*" *urophthalmus* and ex*C. festae*. In both cases, the "junior" species is still a hefty fish!

Herichthys carpintis
(Jordan & Snyder 1899)
Size: 8 inches (20 cm) TL.

Herichthys carpintis
(Jordan & Snyder 1899)
Size: 8 inches (20 cm) TL.

Herichthys bartoni
(Bean 1892)
Size: 8 inches (20 cm) TL.

Herichthys labridens
(Pellegrin 1903)
Size: 10 inches (25 cm) TL.

Herichthys minckleyi
(Kornfield & Taylor 1983)
Size: 7 inches (18 cm) TL.

Herichthys steindachneri
(Jordan & Snyder 1899)
Size: 16 inches (40 cm) TL.

Please see remarks opposite
regarding care and husbandry.

Herichthys cyanoguttatus
BAIRD & GIRARD 1854

Trade Names: Texas cichlid, blue Texas cichlid, Rio Grande perch.

Size: 12 inches (30 cm) TL.

Dietary Notes: An omnivore that likes a lot of plant material in the diet.

Remarks: Native to the lower Rio Grande from Texas into northeast Mexico, this is the only cichlid found naturally within US borders. It can be kept with other native fishes in unheated aquaria. Spawning fish are white in front and black or black barred in back. Other species of *Herichthys* are basically just as easy to care for but they nearly always require a heated aquarium. Ironically, not all species within the group breed as easy as the Texas cichlid, and hobbyists have gone to great lengths to get many of them to spawn for them—sometimes still failing in their efforts.

An adult male *Herichthys carpintis* "Escondido".

Herotilapia

This is a monotypic genus. Its only species is found on the Atlantic slope from Honduras to Costa Rica and on the Pacific slope from Nicaragua to Costa Rica. It is an excellent beginner's cichlid.

Herotilapia multispinosa
(GÜNTHER 1866)

| 7.0 | 7.2 | 7.4 |

Trade Name: Rainbow cichlid.

Size: 4 inches (10 cm) TL.

Dietary Notes: Primarily a detritivore and algivore.

Remarks: Many wonder about the common name for this cichlid, but if you have ever seen one under natural sunlight, you will see how they might have come to be called "rainbow." Their subtle beauty and ease of spawning keep them popular. They are generally peaceful, but can be aggressive when breeding.

Hypsophrys

Another monotypic genus, considered for a while to be *Copora*. The one species shows reverse dichromatism, with more colorful—but much smaller—females. They are unique in laying nonadhesive eggs, which are places in burrows, but in the aquarium they drift around the bottom.

Hypsophrys nicaraguensis
(GÜNTHER 1864)

7.0	7.2	7.4

Trade Names: Nicaraguensis, nic.

Size: 10 inches (25 cm) TL.

Dietary Notes: Truly omnivorous, include plenty of plant material in the diet.

Remarks: Found on the Atlantic slope of Costa Rica and Nicaragua, including Lake Nicaragua, this is a moderately aggressive but flamboyantly colorful cichlid. They do well in small harems of one male to three or four females.

Nandopsis

This genus is a senior synonym of *Parapetenia*. It has now been restricted to the island cichlids of the Greater Antilles in the West Indies. Big bruisers all, these fish, like all North American heroines, can often be kept as single specimens in large cichlid community tanks, but a pair usually cannot. In fact, even keeping a pair in an undivided tank is extremely risky.

All species are basically spangled black and white, but subtle colors and iridescences make them much more beautiful than that monochromatic description would imply.

In 2003 Kullander moved *N. ramsdeni* into "*Cichlasoma*," though it is not clear why. This species is different from other *Nandopsis* species, both in coloration and in the fact that it is the only one not found in brackish as well as freshwater habitats.

A female *Nandopsis haitiensis* guards her fry!

Nandopsis haitiensis
(TEE-VAN 1935)

7.0	7.2	7.4

Trade Name: Black nasty.

Size: 12 inches (30 cm) TL.

Dietary Notes: Largely herbivorous.

Remarks: Found in lakes and streams on the island of Hispaniola, this is a very popular cichlid. Whether this species, compared to its cousins, deserves a name like "black nasty" is a matter of personal opinion—and most likely also one of individual variation among particular specimens.

Nandopsis ramsdeni
(FOWLER 1938)

Size: 12 inches (30 cm) TL.

Dietary Notes: An omnivore.

Remarks: Native to eastern Cuba, where it is called *joturo,* this is a rare cichlid, both in the hobby and in the wild. Jeff Rapps, a well-known cichlid breeder, has kept several pairs of this species for some time and reports that they are very aggressive, that he must use the complete divider method in order to keep them from killing each other.

Nandopsis tetracanthus
(VALENCIENNES 1831)

 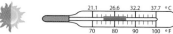

Trade Name: Cuban cichlid.

Size: 14 inches (35 cm) TL.

Dietary Notes: Feeds primarily on invertebrates.

Remarks: Another cichlid endemic to Cuba, *N. tetracanthus* is considerably more available than *N. ramsdeni*. They are a large-growing species that can be very aggressive should a pair set up to spawn. Pairs are best kept in a species-specific, divided aquarium.

Neetroplus

This monotypic genus evokes "neo-*Etroplus*" due to a similarity in fin structure to the etroplines, but the common name "poor man's *Tropheus*" better describes *N. nematopus*, which resembles the Lake Tanganyikan cichlids in body shape, color, and algae-scraping behavior. In breeding dress, with black body and wide white strip, they closely resemble *Tropheus duboisi*.

Neetroplus nematopus
GÜNTHER 1867

Trade Names: Neet, poor man's *Tropheus*.

Size: 5.5 inches (14 cm) TL.

Dietary Notes: Feeds on aufwuchs and algae scraped from rocks and wood.

Remarks: From lakes and rivers on the Atlantic slope of Nicaragua and western Costa Rica, including Lakes Nicaragua and Managua, this is an extremely feisty cichlid when breeding. Spawning dress reverses the normal dark bars on light to a white bar on black.

397

Parachromis

These are the guapote, very large, mean, well-toothed predatory fishes that are prized food fish in their native locales. The "small" species are a foot long, while the guapote poster child, *P. dovii* has a maximum recorded size of 28 inches (72 cm) and 15 pounds (6.8 kg)!

We are talking huge tanks here, and the closer you can get to non-stop water changes, the better. Any fish small enough will be eaten, and some a bit larger may be taken in a couple of bites. Chunks of meaty foods are excellent for these cichlids, but don't forget plant-based foods, too. Aside from the fact that these fish consume plant material in the wild, they regularly prey on fish whose guts are full of algae and vegetation. Although most species are primarily piscivorous, these cichlids also eat large invertebrates and probably wouldn't pass by a suitably sized amphibian, reptile, mammal, or bird if the opportunity was presented.

Although these fish can often be kept in mixed cichlid communities, if a pair forms, the tankmates will be quickly finished off. In addition, many aquarists have had the heartbreak of painstakingly raising a pair to maturity only to lose one (usually but not always the female) to nuptial disharmony, which also amounts to a significant loss of time and money invested. Savvy hobbyists maintain prized pairs in divided tanks.

Parachromis dovii
(GÜNTHER 1864)

| 7.0 | 7.2 | 7.4 |

Trade Names: Wolf cichlid, dovii.

Size: 28 inches (72 cm) TL, usually much smaller.

Dietary Notes: A piscivore.

Remarks: Found on both slopes of Honduras to Costa Rica, this is certainly the prize of the really big cichlid fan. A specimen is often kept in a massive aquarium as an interactive pet, though who owns whom is not always clear. The fish often show a marked bias toward or against particular humans, and they are not beyond showering someone who comes closer than the cichlid wishes…or even biting the hand that feeds them.

Parachromis friedrichsthalii
(HECKEL 1840)

Trade Names: Freddy, yellow jacket cichlid.

Size: 12 inches (30 cm) TL.

Dietary Notes: A piscivore.

Remarks: Found on the Atlantic slope of Mexico to Belize, the popular yellow morph is from Guatemala. It is found in lakes and slow-moving rivers and also enters brackish habitats.

Parachromis loisellei
(BUSSING 1989)

Size: 12 inches (30 cm) TL.

Dietary Notes: A predator.

Remarks: Found on the Atlantic slope from Honduras to Panama and the Pacific slope in Nicaragua, this species prefers muddy and heavily vegetated swamps, where it feeds primarily on terrestrial and aquatic insects.

Parachromis managuensis
(GÜNTHER 1867)

Trade Name: Jaguar cichlid, tiger guapote.

Size: 24 inches (60 cm) TL.

Dietary Notes: A predator of small fishes and macroinvertebrates.

Remarks: Found primarily in eutrophic and oxygen-low habitats on the Atlantic slope of Honduras to Costa Rica, this is another popular but extremely large and aggressive cichlid. Several natural morphs exist in wild populations, largely differing in the size of the splotches.

Parachromis motaguensis
(GÜNTHER 1867)

7.0	7.2	7.4

Trade Names: Jaguar cichlid, red tiger guapote, red mota.

Size: 12 inches (30 cm) TL.

Dietary Notes: A piscivore.

Remarks: Found on both slopes of Guatemala to Honduras, this species prefers faster flowing waters. It comes in several natural morphs, including the prized form with a red base coloration. Many consider it a "dwarf" jaguar cichlid, since it is considerably smaller than *N. managuensis*.

Paraneetroplus

This genus contains four species adapted to life in fast flowing waters. Their range is small, in mountainous rivers on the Atlantic slope of southern Mexico. They are large and quite attractive, and fairly peaceful. A large dark stripe from pectoral to caudal is a distinguishing feature. Their diet should be largely vegetable material.

Paraneetroplus bulleri
REGAN 1905

Size: 10 inches (25 cm) TL.

Dietary Notes: Feeds primarily on algae and aufwuchs.

Remarks: While all large cichlids need large tanks and excellent filtration, those of this genus, being rheophile in habit, are even more demanding of clean, well oxygenated water with a substantial current.

Paratheraps

This genus of about eight species is found in southern Mexico into Guatemala. All are high bodied and laterally compressed, with rounded heads and a broad dark stripe like *Paraneetroplus*. These are species that are included by some in the genus *Vieja*. They are robust and rather aggressive, especially toward conspecifics. All species are true omnivores and require a lot of vegetable matter in the diet.

A young male *Paratheraps synspilus*.

Paratheraps bifasciatus
(Steindachner 1864)
Size: 12 inches (30 cm) TL.

Paratheraps breidhori
Werner & Stawikowski 1987
Size: 10 inches (25 cm) TL.

Paratheraps fenestratus
(Günther 1860)
Size: 10 inches (25 cm) TL.

Paratheraps hartwegi
(Taylor & Miller 1980)
Size: 10 inches (25 cm) TL.

Paratheraps zonatum
(Meek 1905)
Size: 10 inches (25 cm) TL.

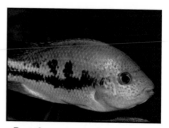

Paratheraps guttulata
(Taylor & Miller 1980)
Size: 10 inches (25 cm) TL.

Please see remarks opposite
for additional information.

Paratheraps synspilus
(HUBBS 1935)

7.0	7.2	7.4

Trade Names: Red head, fire head cichlid, quetzal cichlid.

Size: 18 inches (45 cm) TL.

Dietary Notes: An omnivore.

Remarks: One of the most colorful in the genus, it's also the largest. It is found in a variety of habitats, including slightly brackish ones. From appearance, this species may have been used in the hybridizations to produce flowerhorn cichlids. Most of the species within *Paratheraps* grow to about 10 inches (25 cm) in TL. At this size, they require large aquariums with plenty of swimming room. Water chemistry is not overly critical as long as extremes are avoided. Tankmates should be as large, or larger than these cichlids but not overly aggressive.

Petenia

A monotypic genus from the Atlantic slope of Mexico, Guatemala, and Belize, this cichlid is a specialized piscivore usually found in slow moving waters. Because it is big and a predator, it is quite popular, although it is too large a fish for almost all home aquaria.

Petenia splendida
GÜNTHER 1862

Trade Names: Snook, bay snook, red bay snook.

Size: 20 inches (50 cm) TL.

Dietary Notes: A piscivore.

Remarks: This cichlid is available in two natural morphs: normal greenish bronze and red, which ranges from pinkish white to intense red. It is rather peaceful for such a large cichlid, a common trait of piscivorous species that often surprises people who confuse predation with aggression.

Theraps

The four species in this genus are all rheophilic cichlids from the Atlantic slope of southern Mexico and Guatemala and require extremely clean water. They also appreciate a strong current. They have small, slightly underhung mouths, which are adapted to scraping aufwuchs and algae, their primary foods.

Theraps coeruleus
STAWIKOWSKI & WERNER 1987

7.0	7.2	7.4

Size: 6 inches (15 cm) TL.

Dietary Notes: Feeds on aufwuchs and algae.

Remarks: This rather small cichlid is very pretty with nearly solid blue dorsal fins and cream-colored bodies. Females have a dark blotch in their dorsal fins, which allows them to be easily identified against the males.

Theraps irregularis
GÜNTHER 1862

7.0	7.2	7.4

Size: 8 inches (20 cm) TL.

Dietary Notes: Feeds on aufwuchs and algae.

Remarks: Easily identified by their long, slender bodies with irregular patchwork along their flanks, this is a bold cichlid that comes from rocky, fast moving rivers.

Theraps lentiginosus
(STEINDACHNER 1864)

Size: 10 inches (25 cm) TL.

Dietary Notes: Feeds on aufwuchs and algae.

Remarks: The native habitats of this cichlid are cooler, fast flowing mountain streams where the water is quite hard. Powerheads are useful for providing the oxygen-rich currents such fish require. Like many cichlids, this one demonstrates a dramatic change in coloration when breeding.

Theraps wesseli
MILLER 1996

Size: 8 inches (20 cm) TL.

Dietary Notes: Feeds on aufwuchs and algae.

Remarks: Named for the well-known cichlidophile Rusty Wessel, this cichlid differs in morphology and coloration from its three congeners, and there is speculation it might ultimately be assigned to a different genus.

Thorichthys

This is the firemouth genus, with several variations on a couple of themes in about eight species, with some perhaps to be described. Though heroines in general exhibit opportunistic trophic behaviors, this genus is specialized for sand sifting and detritivory. Like the Geophagini, these small to mid-size cichlids have morphological and behavioral adaptations for taking substrate into the mouth, passing it over gill rakers that capture edible particles, and ejecting the inedible substrate out through the gills. As is typical for detritivores, these fish will eat anything, and they should have a balanced diet of meaty and plant foods.

With all this gular and opercular adaptation and flexibility, these fish have an ideal place to put contrastive coloration to use in threat displays. The eponymous firemouth *Thorichthys meeki* has bright red color with black ocelli on the opercula; thus, when it flares its gills and throat membranes, there is a flash of blood red with two giant eyes. *T. pasionis* uses black instead of red. Aquarists aren't the only ones this impresses, and the behavior is used in both mating and threat displays.

For all these theatrics, these fish are generally peaceful; they rely on bluff and bravado rather than brutishness. They will do well in a community setting, as long as their tankmates are smaller and/or not too aggressive. In a sufficiently large tank more than one pair can establish territories.

They generally display minimal dimorphism; the males have slightly longer fins and slightly more intense coloration. The colors of both sexes intensify at spawning time. Many species have several natural color morphs in different populations, and there are a number of locality-named fish coming in that may be assigned to new species.

413

Thorichthys affinis
(Günther 1862)
Size: 5.5 inches (14 cm) TL.

Thorichthys aureus
(Günther 1862)
Size: 6 inches (15 cm) TL

Thorichthys ellioti
Meek 1904
Size: 5.5 inches (14 cm) TL.

Thorichthys helleri
(Steindachner 1864)
Size: 6 inches (15 cm) TL.

Thorichthys pasionis
(Rivas 1962)
Size: 6 inches (15 cm) TL.

Thorichthys socolofi
(Miller & Taylor 1984)
Size: 5 inches (12 cm) TL.

Please see remarks opposite
regarding care and husbandry.

Thorichthys meeki
BRIND 1918

Trade Names: Firemouth, meeki.

Size: 7 inches (17 cm) TL.

Dietary Notes: A sandsifter.

Remarks: Found on the Atlantic slope in Mexico, Guatemala, and Belize, this is the original firemouth in the hobby, popular for its blood-red throat. Although it has been captive bred for decades, many cichlidophiles are quite excited about some of the wild populations that are being imported. For years, only *T. meeki* was available to hobbyists on a regular basis. Now, with the devotion of cichlidophiles like Rusty Wessel, we have other members of the genus to experience and observe in aquariums. Thankfully, their care and husbandry is simple: clean warm, water and plenty of hiding spots with a varied diet is about all you need for success with these beautiful little cichlids.

Tomocichla

Three species are currently described in this genus. All require pristine water and heavy currents to thrive. They are true omnivores, with plant material required in their diet. They have little sexual dimorphism and are open substrate spawners and extremely devoted parents.

Tomocichla asfraci
ALLGAYER 2002

| 7.0 | 7.2 | 7.4 |

21.1   26.6   32.2   37.7 °C
70   80   90   100 °F

Size: 10 inches (25 cm) TL.
Dietary Notes: An omnivore.
Remarks: New to and still rare in the hobby, this beautiful cichlid comes from the Atlantic slope of Panama. It has a gold background color with red in the fins and rust colored flanks.

Tomocichla sieboldii
(KNER 1863)

Size: 10 inches (25 cm) TL.

Dietary Notes: An omnivore.

Remarks: Found on the Pacific Slope of Costa Rica to Panama, this is a cichlid from fast moving waters that requires high oxygenation. Juveniles are mostly insectivorous, while adults feed primarily on algae and aufwuchs.

417

Tomocichla tuba
(MEEK 1912)

| 7.0 | 7.2 | 7.4 |

Size: 12 inches (30 cm) TL.
Dietary Notes: An omnivore.
Remarks: From the Atlantic slope, Nicaragua to Panama, this rheophilic species is almost wholly herbivorous, feeding on algae, plants, and fruit. Juveniles also take aquatic insects.

Vieja

As mentioned above, in some taxonomies this genus is huge. Here we are following a system that removes most of the species, leaving only three described species in *Vieja*. These are high bodied cichlids, basically light with black markings and specklings, but the iridescent colors of well maintained specimens are strikingly beautiful.

Vieja argentea
(REGAN 1905)

7.0	7.2	7.4

Size: 12 inches (30 cm) TL.

Dietary Notes: An omnivore.

Remarks: From the Atlantic slope of Mexico to Guatemala, this is a largely silver fish with black markings, the most prominent being the large splotch on the caudal peduncle.

Vieja maculicauda
ALLGAYER 1991

| 7.0 | 7.2 | 7.4 |

Trade Name: Blackbelt cichlid.

Size: 10 inches (25 cm) TL.

Dietary Notes: A herbivore.

Remarks: Found in slow flowing waters over mud or sandy substrates on the Atlantic slope from Guatemala to Panama, this cichlid enters brackish and marine habitats. It feeds on detritus, aquatic and terrestrial plants, seeds, and fruits. The red throat and tail are striking.

Vieja regani
(MILLER 1974)

Size: 12 inches (30 cm) TL.

Dietary Notes: Primarily a detritivore.

Remarks: From the Atlantic slope of southern Mexico, this large cichlid lacks the extensive red of *V. maculicauda*, specimens can show considerable blue and red iridescence. There is a natural color variant with a black back.

Afterword

That's Cichlidae. The tome in your hands is a rather large nutshell, but only about a quarter of the described species of cichlids are listed in it. Of course, if we restrict ourselves to the common species in the hobby we've covered a much larger portion. Nevertheless, the book is in some sense unfinished. As it should be. The grand story of Cichlidae is still unfolding, for ichthyologists and for hobbyists.

It seems that every time scientists think they have some facet of cichlid biology right, a new observation or discovery derails them. Whether it's a blind lamprologine, a mouthbrooding heroine, or the possibility of a 30-year speciation, there are always new surprises.

The same is true for cichlidophiles. You could breed a new species of cichlid every week of every year, and you'd be busy for about 50 years. Given the enormous variation in size, form, color, temperament, habits, and reproductive strategies among these fish, such an undertaking would never be boring and repetitive. Aquarists who specialize in cichlids do not have to look any farther than this group for a lifetime of interest, even fascination.

Trying to capture this group of fishes between book covers is, therefore, a frustrating task, yet a rewarding one as well. This is also much like the story of cichlids themselves. They enter a new habitat and speciate furiously, yet whole segments of the family are plunging into extinction even as we try to catalogue them completely.

In a real sense, writing this book has been a matter of chasing the evolution of cichlids around the world. This global pursuit has, I hope, brought this incredible family of fascinating fish into clearer focus for you. Exhausting if not exhaustive, this work has not brought me to satiation, but rather to increased fascination. I hope it does for you, too.

David E. Boruchowitz
January 2006

Bibliography

BOOKS

Axelrod, H.R., et al. (2004): *Dr. Axelrod's Atlas of Freshwater Aquarium Fishes, 10th Edition*. T.F.H. Publications, Inc., New Jersey, United States.

Axelrod, H.R., et al. (2004): *Dr. Axelrod's Mini-Atlas of Freshwater Aquarium Fishes, 3rd Edition*. T.F.H. Publications, Inc., New Jersey, United States.

Brichard, P. (1989): *Pierre Brichard's Book of Cichlids and All the Other Fishes of Lake Tanganyika*. T.F.H. Publications, Inc., New Jersey, United States.

Conkel, D. (1993): *Cichlids of North & Central America*. T.F.H. Publications, Inc., New Jersey, United States.

de Rham, P., J-C. Nourissat (2005): *The Endemic Cichlids of Madagascar*, Association France Cichlid.

Degen, B. (1995): *Wild-Caught Discus*. T.F.H. Publications, Inc., New Jersey, United States.

Glaser, U. and W. Glaser (1996): *Aqualog - South American Cichlids I*. Verlag A.C.S. GmbH, Morfelden-Walldorf, Germany.

Glaser, U. and W. Glaser (1996): *Aqualog - South American Cichlids II*. Verlag A.C.S. GmbH, Morfelden-Walldorf, Germany.

Glaser, U. and W. Glaser (1996): *Aqualog - South American Cichlids III*. Verlag A.C.S. GmbH, Morfelden-Walldorf, Germany.

Konings, A. (1989): *Cichlids From Central America*. T.F.H. Publications, Inc., New Jersey, United States.

Konings, A. (1990): *Ad Konings's Book of Cichlids and All The Other Fishes of Lake Malawi*. T.F.H. Publications, Inc., New Jersey, United States.

Konings, A. (1996): *Back to Nature Guide to Tanganyika Cichlids*. Back to Nature, Jonsered, Sweden.

Lamboj, A. (2004): *The Cichlid Fishes of West Africa*. Birgit Schmettkamp Verlag, Bornheim, Germany.

Loiselle, P.V. (1994): *The Cichlid Aquarium*. Tetra-Press, Melle, Germany.

Staeck, W. and H. Linke (1994): *African Cichlids I: Cichlids From Western Africa*. Tetra-Press, Melle, Germany.

Staeck, W. and H. Linke (1994): *African Cichlids II: Cichlids From Eastern Africa*. Tetra-Press, Melle, Germany.

Staeck, W. and H. Linke (1994): *American Cichlids I: Dwarf Cichlids*. Tetra-Press, Melle, Germany.

Staeck, W. and H. Linke (1994): *American Cichlids II: Large Cichlids*. Tetra-Press, Melle, Germany.

Weidner, T. (2000): *South American Eartheaters*. Cichlid Press, Texas, United States.

ARTICLES

de Rham, Patrick. (1996): *Oxylapia polli*, the Enigmatic Cichlid of the Nosivolo River. Cichlids Yearbook 6. Cichlid Press.

Klett, Vera, A. Meyer. (2002): What, if Anything, is a Tilapia?—Mitochondrial ND2 Phylogeny of Tilapiines and the Evolution of Parental Care Systems in the African Cichlid Fishes. *Molecular Biology and Evolution* 19:865-883.

Konings, A. (1993). A revision of the genus *Sciaenochromis* Eccles & Trewavas, 1989 (Pisces, Cichlidae). The Cichlids

Yearbook, Volume 3: 28-36. Cichlid Press, St. Leon-Rot, Germany; 96 pp.

Nduwarugira, F., Contribution à l'étude du régime alimentaire de *Lobochilotes labiatus* et *Neolamprologus tretocephalus*. Université du Burundi. http://www.geo.arizona.edu/nyanza/nduwarugira.pdf Oldworldcichlids.de. http://oldworldcichlids.com

Plumptre, A.J., Behangana, M., et al. (2003). *The Biodiversity of the Albertine Rift*. Albertine Rift Technical Reports No. 3, 107 pp. http://albertinerift.org/media/file/Biodiversity-8.pdf

Salzburger, W., A. Meyer, et al. (2002). Phylogeny of the Lake Tanganyika Cichlid Species Flock and Its Relationship to the Central and East African Haplochromine Cichlid Fish Faunas. *Syst. Biol.* 51(1):113–135.

Salzburger, W., A. Meyer. (2004). The species flocks of East African cichlid fishes: recent advances in molecular phylogenetics and population. Published online: 20 April, 2004. Springer-Verlag. http://ducksrus.bu.edu/%7Esoren/Salzburger1.pdf

Salzburger, W., T. Mack, et al. (2005). Out of Tanganyika: Genesis, explosive speciation, key-innovations and phylogeography of the haplochromine cichlid fishes. *BMC Evolutionary Biology*, 5:17. http://www.biomedcentral.com/1471-2148/5/17

Sven O Kullander and Swedish Museum of Natural History. (2004). *Guide to the South American Cichlidae*, http://www2.nrm.se/ve/pisces/acara/cm_scitu.shtml, Latest update: 09 April, 2004.

Takahashi, K., Y. Terai, et al. (2001). Phylogenetic Relationships and Ancient Incomplete Lineage Sorting Among Cichlid Fishes in Lake Tanganyika as Revealed by Analysis of the Insertion of Retroposons. *Molecular Biology and Evolution* 18:2057-2066.

Resources

MAGAZINES

Tropical Fish Hobbyist
1 T.F.H. Plaza
3rd & Union Avenues
Neptune City, NJ 07753
Phone: (732) 988-8400
E-mail: info@tfh.com
www.tfhmagazine.com

INTERNET RESOURCES

A World of Fish
www.aworldoffish.com

Aquarium Hobbyist
www.aquariumhobbyist.com

Cichlids.com
www.cichlids.com

**The Cichlid Room
Companion.**
http://www.cichlidae.com

Cichlid Forum
www.cichlid-forum.com

Discus Page Holland
www.dph.nl

**FINS: The Fish Information
Service**
http://fins.actwin.com

Fish Geeks
www.fishgeeks.com

Fish Index
www.fishindex.com

Tropical Resources
www.tropicalresources.net

Water Wolves
http://forums.waterwolves.com

ACADEMIC RESOURCES
AND SOCIETIES

American Cichlid Association
Claudia Dickinson,
Membership Coordinator
P.O. Box 5078
Montauk, NY 11954
Phone: (631) 668-5125
E-mail:
IvyRose@optonline.net
www.cichlid.org

**American Society of
Ichthyologists and
Herpetologists**
Maureen Donnelly, Secretary
Florida International
University
Biological Sciences
11200 SW 8th Street
Miami, FL 33199
Phone: (305) 348-1235
Fax: (305) 348-1986
E-mail: asih@fiu.edu
www.asih.org

Association of Aquarists
David Davis, Membership
Secretary
2 Telephone Road
Portsmouth, Hants, England
PO4 0AY
Phone: 01705 798686

**Canadian Association of
Aquarium Clubs**
Miecia Burden, Membership
Coordinator
142 Stonehenge Pl.
Kitchener, Ontario, Canada
N2N 2M7
Phone: (517) 745-1452
E-mail: mbburden@look.ca
www.caoac.on.ca

**Federation of American
Aquarium Societies**
Jane Benes, Secretary
923 Wadsworth Street
Syracuse, NY 13208-2419
Phone: (513) 894-7289
E-mail: jbenes01@yahoo.com
www.gcca.net/faas

**Society of Systematic
Biologists**
47 Runway Road, Suite G
Levittown, PA 19057-4700
Phone: (800) 821-8312 ext.
117
E-mail: ppagano@taylorand-
francis.com
http://systbiol.org/

Web-based Information
Kocher, T., Adaptive evolution
and Explosive speciation: The
cichlid fish model.
http://hcgs.unh.edu/staff/koch
er/pdfs/Kocher2004.pdf

http://malawicichlids.com/m
    w08011.htm M. K.
    Oliver, PhD.

http://www.hull.ac.uk/cich-
    lids/benthic_gallery.h
    tml G.F. Turner

Subject Index

Index to Scientific Names

445

Acknowledgements

This was of necessity a work based on the work of others. The sheer vastness of Cichlidae makes it impossible to have detailed personal experience with even a majority of species. The research of ichthyologists and expert aquarists on which I relied is reflected in part in the bibliography, but much of their contribution filters through the hobby and becomes part of general knowledge as well. The wide-ranging scope of this book was also supported by observations of aquarists that are also circulated, and this work is partly reflected in the resources listed herein. Additionally, innumerable articles read, presentations heard, and discussions had over the last 40 years or so all combine with my own decades of experience with these fascinating fishes to form the foundation on which this book was built.

A special thanks goes to Brian Scott, editor of this book, who was active in every aspect of its development, from germinal idea to finished product, and whose help and friendship proved invaluable during the entire process.

Photo Credits

Front Cover – Ed Wong (*Cichla orinocensis*)
Back Cover – Morrell Devlin (*Herichthys carpintis* "Escondido"); Ad Konings (*Cyanthopharynx furcifer*); Oliver Lucanus (*Hemichromis* sp.)
Title Page – Pablo Tepoot (*Metriaclima zebra* "OB Albino")

The author would like to extend a special thanks to the following individuals who graciously provided photographs for inclusion in this work…and to anyone else whose name might have been inadvertently omitted from the list.

Aaron Norman	Klaus Paysan
Ad Konings	Laif DeMason
Ariel Bornstein	M.P. & C. Piednoir (Aqua Press)
Brian M. Scott	Mark Smith
David Hansen	Melanie Stiassny
Ed Wong	Morrell Devlin
Glen S. Axelrod	Oliver Lucanus
Hans-Joachim Richter	Pablo Tepoot
Hans Mayland	Patrick De Rham
Heiko Bleher	Pierre Brichard
Jeff Rapps	Raymond Tesoriero
K.P. Devlin	Stan Sung
Kevin Bauman	Uwe Werner

Additional photos were provided by the photo archives of T.F.H. Publications, Inc.